Ford at Dagenham

The Rise and Fall of Detroit in Europe

David Burgess-Wise is the author of some 30 books, including two specially commissioned centennial histories of major British manufacturers – Daimler Century, the story of Britain's oldest motor manufacturing company, written in conjunction with Lord Montagu of Beaulieu, and Vauxhall, A Century in Motion, published in December 2003. His latest title is Brighton Belles, published in 2006, and he has also translated the award-winning French history of the Delage marque Delage – la Belle Voiture Française into English for 2007 publication.

He is a member of the Guild of Motoring Writers and Editor of Aston, the journal of the Aston Martin Heritage Trust. Aston has won the Society of Automotive Historians' Richard and Grace Brigham Award for 2005. This award is given annually to recognize the periodical judged to have given the best treatment of automotive history over all issues in the preceding year.

In 2006 David was invited to join the Advisory Council of the National Motor Museum.

As European Consultant to the American connoisseur's motoring magazine Automobile Quarterly, his feature "Bentley at Le Mans" won David a Silver Award in the 2002 International Automotive Media Awards. He contributes regularly to Autocar, The Automobile, Classic Cars for Sale, Octane and The Daily Telegraph; his long-running Telegraph series "A Good Idea at the Time" won David a 1995 Renault Journalist of the Year award.

Ford promised the 'greatest thrill in motoring' to purchasers of the new V8 in 1932. It could certainly match most contemporary sports cars in straight line acceleration, though its brakes and steering were not up to sports car standards.

The greatest thrill in motoring.

Ford at Dagenham

The Rise and Fall of Detroit in Europe

David Burgess-Wise

DB
PUBLISHING

First published in Great Britain in 2001 by
The Breedon Books Publishing Company Limited
Breedon House, 3 The Parker Centre, Derby, DE21 4SZ.
Paper back edition 2007

This edition published in Great Britain in 2012 by
The Derby Books Publishing Company Limited,
3 The Parker Centre, Derby, DE21 4SZ.

Acknowledgements

My grateful thanks to the following who - past and present - helped with
this book: Fran Chamberlain and Jim Fowler of Ford Photographic Services,
Walter Hayes, Sir Patrick Hennessy, Allen Barke, Sir Rowland Smith, Maurice
Buckmaster, Sir Terence Beckett, Harry Calton, Sid Wheelhouse, Ron Hickman,
Colin Neale, Charles J.Thompson, John Frayling, Fred Ferguson, Peter
Kennedy, Sam Roberts, Les Geary, Dennis Roberts, George Baggs, Bill
Camplisson, Bernard Ford, David A Hayward, David Leon.

ISBN 978-1-78091-136-6

Printed and bound by Copytech (UK) Limited, Peterborough.

CONTENTS

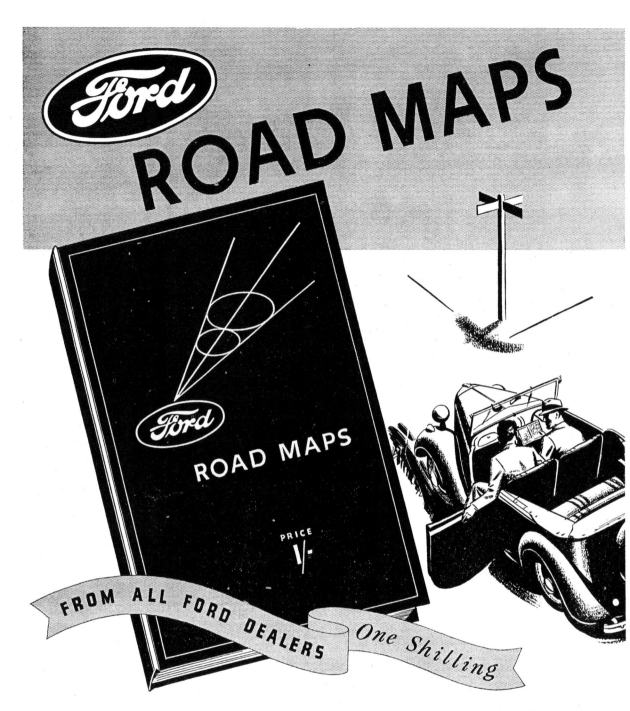

ROAD MAPS

Ford ROAD MAPS

PRICE 1/-

FROM ALL FORD DEALERS — One Shilling

The book, which comprises 64 map-sections, covering the whole of Great Britain, measures 8½ x 5½ ins., and is strongly bound in blue cloth. All the main sections are on a scale of 8 miles to an inch. The latest Ministry of Transport road-numbers are adopted, "A" roads being shown in red and "B" in green, while the mileages between towns are shown in blue.

The sections are arranged from West to East, starting from the North of Scotland, and finishing in the South, so that any desired map can be found without difficulty. London is covered in a series of eight sections, on a scale of 1 mile to an inch.

The arrangement of marginal notes to facilitate transfer from one map to another is interesting. In most maps the page on which the section is continued is given, but difficulty arises in picking up the continuation of the road on the new sheet.

In the Ford Book of Maps, each road ending in the margin is numbered with the official road-number, together with the name of the next largest town. A glance down the margin of the new section enables the road-number to be picked out without difficulty.

Copies are obtainable from Ford dealers : Price 1s.

FORD MOTOR COMPANY LIMITED, DAGENHAM, ESSEX

Black Market: Yesterday

A hundred and fifty years ago, many a profitable cargo of lace and brandy slipped past the Customs over those lonely Dagenham marshes. Black forbidden imports! Now those same marshes are dedicated to a better purpose. For on them stands the great Ford factory—producing cars, trucks and tractors on an unprecedented scale for Britain's export drive. Over these same waters, where once the smugglers' schooner crept in at midnight, the Ford jetty now swings its cranes and a continuous stream of cargo ships ride out, laden with Ford products and bound for Scandinavia, Spain, Turkey, Iceland, Africa, Pacific Islands and the other overseas markets which are eagerly waiting. During the last year, these export cargoes have broken all records — and the volume is increasing.

 OF DAGENHAM

CARS · VANS · TRUCKS · TRACTORS

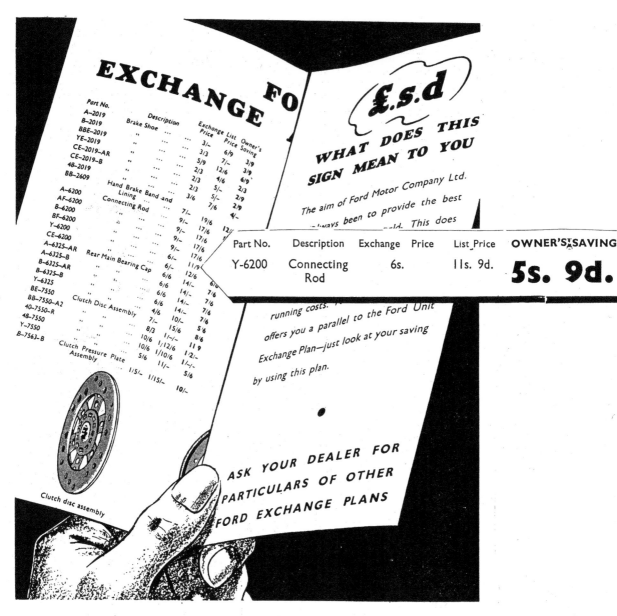

Part No.	Description	Exchange Price	List Price	Owner's Saving
Y-6200	Connecting Rod	6s.	11s. 9d.	**5s. 9d.**

A TYPICAL EXAMPLE OF THE SAVING
YOU MAKE UNDER THE

FORD *UNIT* EXCHANGE PLAN

Factory-reconditioned units not only effect a saving in cost and time, but ensure that reconditioning is carried out with genuine Ford parts.

Reconditioned units are given the same attention and rigid inspection as new components, thus insuring the user against any reconditioning which will not give satisfactory service.

Ask your Dealer for the Booklet illustrated above, containing particulars and complete list of exchangeable parts

FORD MOTOR COMPANY LIMITED · DAGENHAM · ESSEX

INTRODUCTION

THOUGH it happened over 50 years ago, I still have vivid memories of my first visit to Dagenham, when I was a second-former at Purley County Grammar School. The drama of the foundry, where red-hot metal was poured into sand-filled moulds from which cylinder blocks and crankshafts were presently liberated in a cloud of steam, made a lasting impression.

Dagenham had already had had quite an influence on my life: the first car that I t can remember riding in as a child just after World War Two was my uncle's little green Model Y Ford "Bonnie". That gave way to a terminally dull Hillman Minx of which I can only recall that it was painted funereal black. Thankfully, as new cars became more readily available on the home market, Minnie the Minx was replaced by a new Ford Consul painted Wells Fawn. Inevitably, it became known as "Connie". I remember the excitement of seeing the magic "60" come up on its half moon-shaped speedometer as we headed north from Brighton, but I had no idea then that my lifelong passion for cars would one clay find me working for Ford.

I joined Ford as assistant editor of Ford Times magazine in 1972, midway through the Cortina years and at the end of the Zephyr/Zodiac era. Later – after the corporate beancounters had killed off Ford Times as a "cost saving" during the first oil shock of 1974 – I transferred to public affairs. The history and heritage of the Ford Motor Company fascinated me. Both during my time in public affairs and later, when I ran Ford's European Corporate History Office for the late Walter Hayes – public affairs legend and confidant of Henry Ford II – I was privileged to talk to many of the men who had shaped Ford's past and present history. Long chats with Sir Patrick Hennessy at his Theydon Boi& home, accompanied by generous glasses of Irish whiskey, and later on, lunchtime sessions with bis former assistant Allen Barke, gave me a flavour of what it had been like to work at Ford in the interwar years. I even met a nonagenarian who 60 years before had surveyed the wasteland that was the Dagenham marshes for Ford before the first pile was driven.

This is my tribute to a factory that changed Britain's motoring history – I'm glad I knew it in its glory days.

David Burgess-Wise
April 2005

Chapter One

PRELUDE: FROM LONDON TO MANCHESTER

ORD and Dagenham: to the British motorist, the two names are inextricably linked. Over 70 years Ford's Thames-side plant produced millions of cars, trucks and tractors that became part of motoring lore – Popular, Prefect, Anglia, Pilot, Cortina, Zephyr, Thames and Fordson. Its place in Ford history seemed so sure that when in 1996 the worldwide Ford empire built its 250 millionth vehicle, Dagenham was the natural choice to make it. So it came as a shock when it was announced that car production at Dagenham would cease in 2002, although the factory's role as a major supplier of power units to Ford's European plants was assured.

The road to Dagenham was a long and fascinating one, and it began in a Detroit tailor's fitting room in June 1903. Charles H. Bennett, president of the Daisy Air Rifle Company, had dropped in to have a new suit fitted. As the tailor worked, Bennett told him about the new Oldsmobile car that he was going to buy.

A head popped out of the next changing booth. 'Pardon me,' said the stranger, 'Have you heard about the new Ford car?' The speaker was Frank Malcomson, whose well-to-do coal merchant cousin Alexander Malcomson was bankrolling the new marque, which had just gone on the market.

Henry Ford first visited Britain in 1912. When he landed in Plymouth he bought a Rolls-Royce ('the next best thing to a Ford') and later went to Ireland to visit the family homestead at Ballinascarty, County Cork, which his father had left in 1847 to seek his fortune in America.

Bennett was taken to see the car's designer, Henry Ford, and tried the Ford Model A on the road. With twin cylinders and wheel steering, it was a far more substantial machine than the single-cylinder, tiller-steered 'Curved Dash' Oldsmobile, and Bennett was enchanted. He pledged $5,000 to help launch the new Ford Motor Company, and when Ford asked for help in marketing his car outside the US, Bennett recommended a New York export agent named Robert M. Lockwood, who handled overseas sales of Daisy air rifles.

A short while later, Lockwood had a visitor from England. Arthur Shippey was managing director of Shippey Brothers American Manufacturers Direct Supply Agency, which handled British sales of the Toledo and Milwaukee steam cars, Pope petrol cars and Merkel motor cycles. He thought the new Ford car had potential, and took two back to England to exhibit on the stand of a subsidiary company, the American Motor Car Agency, at the March 1904 Cordingley Show in the Agricultural Hall, Islington. Also exhibiting a Ford car was the British Duryea Company, an offshoot of the company which had been the first in America to offer series-produced cars for sale. The Duryea Company was certainly the first to advertise the newcomer ('If you can't afford a Duryea, get a Ford') and offered the new make as a lower-priced adjunct to the British-built Duryea, which sold for £425 against the £195 asked for the Ford.

The new car caught the attention of Aubrey Blakiston, who was setting up a new sales agency. He ordered a dozen Model A Fords and traded shares in his new company for a 16-year lease of the American Motor Car Agency's showrooms in Shippey's Central Emporium at 117 Long Acre, a London centre of the coach-building and motor trade.

When Blakiston organised a lunch at the Albemarle Club in London to discuss the future of his company, his guests included Herbert Marmaduke Stourton (a relative of Lord Stourton & Mowbray), Anthony Hasslacher (a partner in the Deinhard wine company whose wife was related to Blakiston), banker C.W. Russell, R.A. Houghton and a young 'motor expert' named Percival Perry, who had been called in to give a professional opinion on the Ford car.

Perry had literally been in at the birth of the British motor industry, for in 1896 he had left his home in Birmingham to seek his fortune in London at the Holborn Viaduct headquarters of the Great Horseless Carriage Company, lynch-pin of the ambitious plans of the notorious company promoter Harry J. Lawson to monopolise the infant British motor industry by acquiring all available 'master patents'. It was a useful grounding, although Perry left the already crumbling Lawson empire in 1898 to set up as a motor accessory dealer.

Inside the Ford factory in Detroit around 1907, when Model N Fords were being turned out at the rate of 45 cars a day, six days a week. Model N, which sold in Britain for £120, was the first Ford to catch on with the British car-buying public.

Percival Perry's wife at the wheel of a 1912 Manchester-built Model T, which retailed at £135 ('neat folding dickey seat £1 extra'). By then the cars were being imported in chassis form and bodied by a local firm named Scott Brothers, which was taken over by Ford in 1912.

The Central Motor Car Company was incorporated on 18 November 1904, with a capital of £10,000, to take over the Blakiston syndicate as a going concern. Although the Ford was optimistically advertised as 'America's Favorite Car', Blakiston had a hard time selling even that first dozen. Roland Philip, appointed company secretary on 19 April 1905, recalled that 'the dozens of times when disaster stared us in the eyeball, when the inconvenient dozen or so Model As (first edition) would not leave us, but returned inevitably to be polished and placed in the white showroom for another day, would have undermined the courage of the hardiest!'

Unconfirmed legend says that the first British customer was a Liverpool doctor specialising in the treatment of wealthy lunatics, a legend perhaps corroborated by a letter received by Ford in 2003 from a Mr Charles Lewis stating that family tradition averred that his ancestor, a Liverpool motor agent named Donkin, had sold the first Ford car in England.

But sales were still minute, remembered Roland Philip: 'Recollections of visitors to the showroom conjure up pictures of those who called to examine our only model and, never pausing in their stride, walked round it and passed straight out into Long Acre. Again, a day when we sold a 14 hp Model F, or another occasion when we had two genuine enquiries on the same morning, left us delirious.'

In the summer of 1906 Blakiston resigned and Perry became managing director. He travelled to Detroit to ask Henry Ford for greater works support. Though this was not forthcoming, Perry stayed with Ford's family, and recalled having to race young Edsel Ford for the bathroom each morning!

Helpfully, Gordon McGregor, head of Ford-Canada – which owned the exclusive right to 'make and sell automobiles within the Dominion and British Colonies' – waived his claim to the United Kingdom market with the immortal words: 'The rest of the British Empire is enough for me!'

The Central Motor Car Company struggled on, selling the more expensive Russell and SCAR cars alongside the Ford, but early in 1907 Perry put Central into liquidation and formed Perry, Thornton & Schreiber Ltd with two friends.

The change had come at precisely the right moment: priced at only £120, the new four-cylinder Ford Model N proved popular, and 50 were sold in the new company's first year. Although the Model N was only available from Detroit with two-seater bodywork, Perry astutely tailored it to the British market by fitting four-seat and landaulette coachwork.

During 1908, Perry, Thornton & Schreiber moved into new premises in Westminster Bridge Road. There were just seven employees – four men and three boys.

When the famous Model T went into production in October 1908, eight of the first batch to be built were shipped to London for the new car's world show debut on the Perry, Thornton & Schreiber stand at London's Olympia motor exhibition.

Early in 1909, Perry left the company after falling out with Thornton and Schreiber. He travelled to America to see Henry Ford and discuss his views on the potential for Ford in Britain. While he was there, Ford's company secretary James Couzens arrived in Britain to examine the situation for himself. As a result of his recommendations, Ford withdrew the agency from Thornton and Schreiber, which went into liquidation as a result. Henry Ford then formed a London branch of the Ford Motor Company and invited Perry to head it. Its offices were at 55–59 Shaftesbury Avenue, in London's West End.

Cars for the London company were landed at Vauxhall Wharf, packed in crates. Their wheels had been removed to reduce shipping dimensions. The crate containing the first T to arrive after the formation of the new company was accidentally dropped by the unloading crane, bending the car's axle, which had to be straightened in a garage in Wardour Street. The great advantage of the vanadium steel used in Model T construction was that it could be straightened cold, whereas conventional steel needed heating before it could be bent.

Both Perry and Ford felt that the British market had great potential, and so the decision to manufacture in Britain was taken. As a major part of this scheme, the Ford Motor Company (England) Ltd was established on 29 March 1911, the first Ford company to be set up outside North America. Share capital was £1,000 divided into 200 ordinary shares of £5 each, of which Henry Ford held 117. Directors of the company were Henry Ford, James Couzens, John Dodge and Percival Perry. Perry decided to site the factory in Manchester, open to ocean-going freight since the opening of the Manchester Ship Canal in 1894. He took over a disused tramcar factory on Britain's first trading estate, Trafford Park, to the south of Manchester.

After the factory had been renovated and production machinery installed, hand

Testing Model T chassis outside the Trafford Park works, which had originally been built by a company named Dick Kerr, which built tramcars and railway carriages for the London Underground.

picked members of Ford's London staff were taken north in a specially-chartered train on Saturday 21 October 1911, worked through the Sunday and assembled the first British built Ford car on Monday 23 October.

To save on shipping cost, cars arrived at Manchester from Detroit in knocked-down form in packing crates and were transferred the short distance from the docks to the factory on railway trucks. As production increased, components were bulk-shipped, specially-adapted freighters being used as floating parts depots.

Chassis were built up on trestles until the wheels were fitted, then pushed into the final assembly shop for the coachwork to be added. Manchester started building its own bodies – more suited to British taste – in 1912, when a local coachbuilder was taken over by the company.

Ford production methods of breaking down the manufacture of a vehicle into simple repetitive tasks made it possible for unskilled men to build car bodies, as each component was pre-cut in the woodworking shop and numbered, before being assembled on jigs.

Even painting the bodywork was 'de-skilled'. Paint was flowed on to the bare metal by gravity, through wide nozzles fed from an overhead tank, then dried in a huge gas oven that could hold a dozen bodies.

The Trafford Park Factory revolutionised local working practice, for not only did it offer higher wages than other firms in the area – 10d or 1s 3d (4p or 6.25p) per hour for skilled men and 8½d (3.5p) unskilled - but employees were taken on as 'handymen', not 'tradesmen', so that they could be transferred from one job to another rather than being laid off. This system was modified in 1914, when a flat rate of 1s 3d for shop floor workers was inaugurated in conjunction with a 48-hour week, with up to 4s (20p) for skilled toolmakers. This 'Profit-Sharing Plan' would be the ruin of Ford-Britain, declared the press...

While early American Model Ts had been available in a limited choice of colours, in Britain all cars were painted the same. All 1912 cars were blue, and in 1913 they were green with black wings. In 1914 cars were to have been chocolate brown, but

Native workers push a damaged Model T to a repair depot in the Middle East, where the Ford's role during World War One was crucial. 'The only cars suitable for desert warfare,' declared Lawrence of Arabia, 'are the Model T Ford and the Rolls-Royce Silver Ghost.'

only one prototype was painted when Detroit decreed that all bodies were to be black.

The introduction of the first-ever moving assembly conveyor in Ford's Highland Park factory in Detroit had increased the speed of production so much that black Japan enamel was the only finish that would dry quickly (and thickly) enough to keep pace. Within a few months, a moving conveyor was in operation at Trafford Park and at its fastest rate could produce 21 chassis an hour. By 1914 annual production was 8,300 cars and the Model T Ford outsold the next five biggest British marques combined.

Trafford Park's meteoric progress was not halted by World War One, as 30,000 Model T troop carriers, water carriers, ambulances and munitions carriers were supplied to the government. Lawrence of Arabia said that the Model T and the Rolls-Royce Silver Ghost were the only two cars suitable for desert warfare. The factory's mass-production skills were also used to manufacture shell casings.

Britain needed to grow more food to beat the German submarine blockade, and Perry – appointed Assistant Controller of the government's Agricultural Machinery Department – persuaded Ford to build a tractor factory at Cork in southern Ireland, from where in 1847 Henry Ford's father William had taken ship to seek his fortune in North America. However, the Cork factory (which, like its American counterpart, was personally owned by Henry Ford and his son Edsel) did not start production until eight months after the end of the war, so all the 'Fordson' tractors received during the hostilities came from the US.

In 1917 Perry became Deputy Controller of Mechanical Warfare at the Ministry of Munitions and was knighted for his war work the following year.

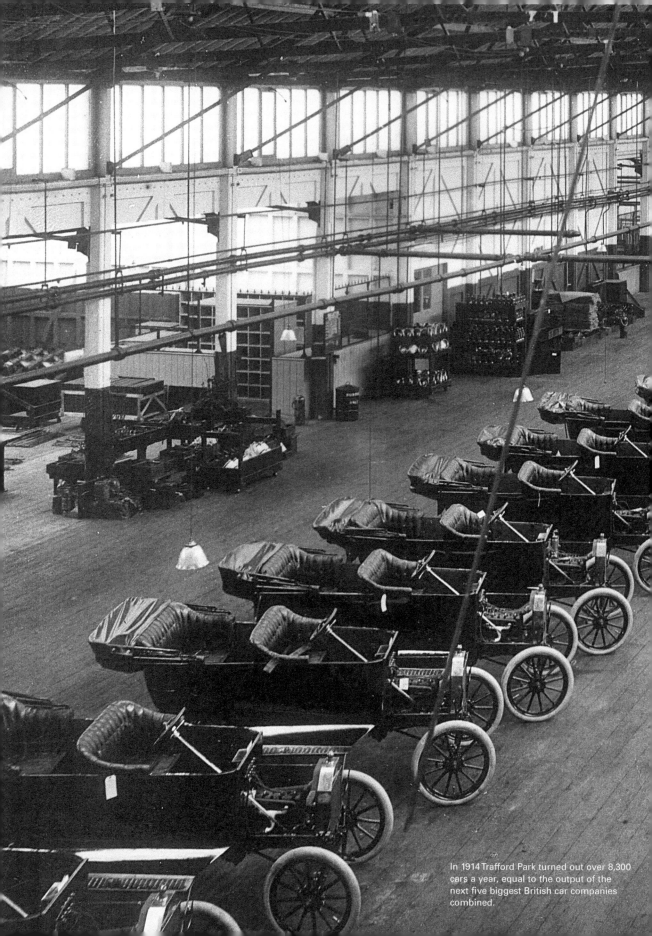

In 1914 Trafford Park turned out over 8,300 cars a year, equal to the output of the next five biggest British car companies combined.

Henry Ford's brief insistence in 1919 that all Model Ts worldwide should be built with left-hand drive led to many accidents in right-hand-drive Britain. Here an early 'piggy-back' Model T trailer operated by International Motors of Brook Green, Hammersmith, London, rescues one of the victims.

Although Ford-Britain had contributed more vehicles to the country's war effort than any other manufacturer, there were still many who declared that the company's products were not English and refused to buy Manchester-built Ford cars on those grounds.

The end of the war brought new problems: there was insufficient land around the Trafford Park factory to accommodate future expansion, and the search for an alternative production site began. Before war broke out, Perry had bought land with deep-water frontage – one of Henry Ford's prerequisites for a factory site – at Millbrook, Southampton, 'with the intention of erecting factories at a cost of £350,000 and a pier or jetty going out to deep water, whereby they would have been two miles by water from the docks'. However, the proposal fell foul of internal Detroit politics and a block was put on development. During the war, the Southampton Corporation had already compulsorily purchased 21 acres of the Ford land on which to build an isolation hospital. Ford protested the acquisition, and the case went to court in 1922, claiming £12,804 in compensation. However, the arbitrator only awarded Ford £5,500 damages from the Corporation, which also had to pay the hearing fee. Each party also

The standard Model T chassis was capable of taking all kinds of bodywork, like this open-sided rural bus.

had to pay its own costs. Eventually, the rest of the site was sold to Southampton Corporation for £3,500 in 1926, becoming the berth of the great Cunard White Star liners in the 1930s.

Ford, wrapped up in his plans to buy out all the shareholders in the Ford Motor Company, was now dealing with Perry through his deputies Knudsen and Klingensmith. There was a clash of personalities and Perry resigned in May 1919. He took the salaried post of managing director of Henry Ford & Son Ltd in Cork but had to step down on health grounds in September.

In April 1920 Perry and Noel Mobbs of the Pytchley Autocar Company raised £7 million to buy the 600-acre Slough Motor Transport Depot, established in 1918 as a central repair depot for military vehicles, and the thousands of military vehicles still awaiting repatriation in France. Astonishingly, the deal also included every vehicle that became surplus to government requirements over the next two years. Perry and Mobbs set up the Slough Trading Company, built 10,000 functioning cars and lorries out of 15,000 wrecks and auctioned them, creaming off much of the post-war demand for motor transport.

By the end of 1920 they had sold £5.125 million worth of war surplus and developed the site as the Slough Trading Estate. In 1922 Perry retired to the tiny Channel Island of Herm, buying the lease from novelist Compton Mackenzie.

With Perry gone, the Manchester company settled into a slow decline under a rapid succession of American managers unable to stem declining sales, penalised by the protectionist 1920 Motor Car Act. Aimed at large-bore American imports, this taxed cars on piston area at the rate of £1 per rated horsepower, which put the utilitarian Manchester-built Model T – rated at 22hp – on a par with such costly cars as the 3-litre Bentley.

The Trafford Park management and part of the 3,000-strong workforce crowd round to celebrate the production in April 1925 of the 250,000th Manchester-built Model T. Works superintendent V. Perini, on the left in the pale suit, looks on proudly.

King George V and Queen Mary inspect the 250,000th Manchester-built Model T on the Ford stand at the British Empire Exhibition at Wembley, where a 60-foot-long chain conveyor manned by 23 Ford workers turned out a Model T every 20 minutes.

A fascinating 'might-have-been' arrived out of the blue on Henry Ford's desk in July 1920, when Sir Herbert Austin, whose Longbridge company in Birmingham was also in trouble, wrote and asked point-blank: 'Would an alliance between the Ford Motor Company and our concern appeal to you? Do you, from your point of view, think the scheme could be made mutually advantageous?'

Austin admitted that he had previously tried unsuccessfully to amalgamate with General Motors, but added: 'I am still of the opinion that we, as the largest British manufacturers of automobiles and agricultural tractors, would be more secure in an amalgamation with one of the leading American firms than to be in strong competition with them.' Henry's response, when it came, could hardly have been briefer: 'Mr Ford does not feel inclined to entertain any proposition such as your

Apart from its obsolescent wood-spoked wheels, the 1926 Model T range looked very much like any other popular British make. Beneath the smart exterior, however, the mechanical mix was pure 1908, with a two-speed transmission and brakes on the rear wheels only.

letter sets forth,' wrote his secretary, E.G. Liebold.

Despite the pressure put on Ford sales by the horsepower tax, the search for a new factory site went on, impelled by the creation of the Irish Free State in 1922. This effectively turned the Cork plant, whose foundry supplied castings to Trafford Park, into a foreign company.

The final stage of the British Model T in 1927 saw the adoption of welded-spoke wire wheels with pressed steel centres that gave the false impression that Ford had at last adopted front wheel brakes.

Components from Cork – which Ford-Britain took over from Henry Ford in April 1927, paying almost $2 million for the privilege – were subject to a 22.2 per cent import duty, adding an unacceptable burden to the production costs of the Model T.

Despite the slump in sales, employment at Trafford Park was still sought after, as Ford continued to pay higher wages than other companies in the Manchester area. One hopeful employee recalled being picked out of a queue of maybe a hundred men all seeking a job with Ford because his prime physical condition, hardened by cycling over the Peaks and playing rugby, made him stand out as someone well-suited to the repetitive rigours of life on the production line.

On secondment, Edward Grace, manager of the Cork plant, motored through England seeking a suitably large site for a new British plant. It had to have deep-water berthing and good road and railway links. His preliminary list of sites ran to several pages, but in 1923 he settled on a marshy site by the Thames near the village of Dagenham in Essex. In May 1924 an initial 295 acres was bought from Samuel Williams & Co, owners of Dagenham Dock, for £150,000, followed by purchases of adjoining parcels of land which would bring the total up to some 600 acres by the mid-1930s. But with Ford sales still hamstrung by the high road tax, the company delayed starting construction at Dagenham.

Meanwhile, Ford's share of the English market continued to slip, with Morris replacing Ford as UK sales leader in 1924, even though advances in paint technology had enabled the Model T to be offered in 'Empire Grey, Orriford Lake or Cobalt Blue' instead of the universal black. At a basic price of £120, the Model T was considerably cheaper than the 'Bullnose' Morris. But beneath her 'Roaring Twenties' skin, the 'Tin Lizzie' was still a 1908 girl at heart, with brakes on the rear wheels only, a hand-controlled throttle and an idiosyncratic pedal-operated two-speed transmission.

Chapter Two

A DETROIT IN MINIATURE

IN 1927, stubborn old Henry Ford finally realised that his obsolescent 'Universal Car' could not go on any longer, and Model T production was wound down worldwide after some 16 million had been built. Amazingly, although there had been various experiments with new powerplants in the company's headquarters in the Detroit suburb of Dearborn, work on the Model T's successor did not begin until the summer of 1927.

Trafford Park built its 301,980th and last Model T – a van – in August 1927 and set about switching over to the new Model A, launched at the end of the year. A smaller 14.9hp engine was offered in addition to the standard 24hp offering, but as it was still larger than any of its rivals' power units, it failed to stem the falling sales of Ford cars.

The launch of the long overdue new model saw Henry Ford taking stock of his European companies. He had already rejected an approach by Sir Herbert Austin in 1926 that proposed a joint venture between Austin and Ford on the English market, for he planned something altogether more ambitious. Ford proposed that his British company should be a Detroit in miniature, a virtually self-sufficient manufacturing colossus supplying and controlling a chain of 11 European assembly plants. Even so, when he paid one of his rare visits to England in the spring of 1928, travelling under the alias 'Mr Robinson', it was as much to buy exhibits for the museum he was building near his Rouge Plant in the Detroit suburb of Dearborn as to review the future of Ford business in Britain.

Ford himself described the main aim of his visit as 'just meeting people', though in reality he wanted to meet just one man – Sir Percival Perry. Ford wanted a competent chief to implement his ambitious '1928 Plan', and, as far as he was concerned, Perry was the only choice.

Henry Ford's visit to Britain was a triumphal progress from the moment he and his wife Clara stepped off the White Star liner *Majestic* at Southampton and were met by the mayor, Mrs Foster-Welch. Early in the first morning of his stay in London, Ford went down to Essex to inspect the Dagenham site.

The Fords were entertained to dinner at the Savoy by the American Society, where the guest list, a remarkable cross-section of British society, included the American

Ambassador and the Lord Mayor of London, Gordon Selfridge, the Dean of St Paul's and such luminaries of the motoring world as Captain Malcolm Campbell and Viscount Curzon (later Lord Howe).

The Savoy was also the venue for a meeting between Henry Ford and Sir Percival Perry, where the Englishman was asked whether he would consider taking the helm of the reformed British Ford company.

Lady Astor invited the Fords to spend the second weekend of their stay at Cliveden, and almost as soon as they arrived, King George V and Queen Mary arrived from Windsor in their huge royal Daimler. The Fords had tea with the king and queen, and talked with them for a couple of hours.

Sir Percival Perry, happily retired in his Channel Island retreat, was initially reluctant to rejoin Ford, but a visit to Detroit soon changed his mind.

The next morning Henry Ford was received by the Prince of Wales at St James's Palace and four days later ex-premier David Lloyd George entertained Ford to lunch at the House of Commons. Lloyd George told Ford that he had long used a Fordson tractor on his farm at Churt (and later claimed Ford had offered to give him a new one. Ford didn't recall having said any such thing, but asked Manchester to put a tractor together from spares and give it to the politician).

During the third week of his stay, Henry Ford visited Oxford and drove out to Cowley to pay a surprise visit to the works of his British company's biggest rival, William Morris. Sadly, Morris was out, but another director of the company showed Ford round the factory.

Toward the end of his visit, Ford visited Trafford Park, collecting various industrial artefacts – including a horsedrawn steam fire engine from Warwick and two huge beam engines built in 1796 and 1812 – and finally left London on May Day, visiting Lord Montagu in his New Forest home at Beaulieu before boarding the liner home at Southampton.

'Mr & Mrs Robinson', alias Henry and Clara Ford, arrive in Southampton aboard the *Majestic* to inspect the Dagenham site and scour the Midlands for exhibits for the planned Ford Museum at Dearborn.

Waiting to see him off was Percival Perry, although at that point he was still undecided about whether to rejoin Ford. However, a few days later the post brought an invitation from Henry and his son Edsel Ford to visit them in their Dearborn headquarters to discuss the project.

'Have nothing to do with those Fords!' admonished Perry's mother-

Looking south-east into Kent from the Dagenham Jetty site in July 1929. The marshy terrain was partly occupied by rubbish tips where London's waste was dumped or burned, and partly by rough grazing where the local children used to play.

Henry Ford and his son Edsel study a scale model of their mighty Rouge Plant in Dearborn. Dagenham was planned as the European counterpart of this self-sufficient manufacturing empire.

in-law before he sailed, but once in Dearborn Perry ignored her and readily accepted the task of developing Ford's European empire. To take charge of the manufacturing side of Ford of Britain – initially in Manchester, then at the plant which was to be built beside the Thames at Dagenham, he recruited A.R. (Rowland) Smith, whose experience in the motor industry went back to the early years of the century. As a teenager Smith had left his family home in Kent and travelled to Coventry to seek his fortune in the motor industry, living in a tent on

June 1929, and work has already begun on the Dagenham site, which had to be stabilised by driving concrete piles into the marshy soil.

common land to save the cost of lodgings. He recalled that when he went out testing single-cylinder Humberette cars in the early 1900s, he was often overtaken by pedal cycles, which were faster.

From 1912 Rowland Smith worked for the Russa Engineering Company, which handled Ford sales in India. In around 1923 he returned to England and joined Ford at Trafford Park, but when his ambition to be assistant plant manager was blocked in 1927, he resigned and went to Standard as works manager.

When Perry first asked him to return to Ford, Smith refused. However, when Perry assured Smith he would have a free hand to change and improve Ford's British manufacturing operation, he accepted immediately.

May 1929 and the first pile is in place, crowned by 11-year-old Henry Ford II, with Edsel Ford *(left)* and Sir Percival Perry as supporters.

Another brilliant young man who joined the staff at Trafford Park at around this time was a red-headed Irishman named Patrick Hennessy. After war service, he had taken a job in the foundry of the company's new Cork tractor plant 'to build up my muscles for playing rugby'!

Hennessy's innate talent ensured his rapid promotion via the post of 'roadman' (travelling representative) to service manager, and in 1928 – after saving a huge tractor order from Russia from potential collapse – he was transferred to England and given control of Ford's purchasing department. This had hitherto operated on a 'horse trading' method of determining the price of bought-in components by simply splitting the difference between what the supplier asked and what the purchase manager was prepared to pay. Hennessy initiated a scientific costing system that enabled the company to keep an unrivalled grip on purchasing from outside suppliers.

Edsel Ford looks as though he's heard it all before as Sir Percival Perry declares that it will take two-and-a-half years to build the Dagenham plant, which will employ 15,000 people and export 200,000 cars a year.

The third member of a triumvirate of gifted managers which would ensure the long-term success of the new organisation was Stanford Cooper, a young accountant who had joined Trafford Park after World War One and developed a new procedure for controlling manufacturing costs. His abilities ensured that when the new Ford Motor Company was floated in 1928, he was appointed company secretary.

The new Ford Motor Company Ltd was successfully floated in December 1928 and eager investors quickly snapped up its issued capital of £7 million. Indeed, many of the purchasers were Americans, who had never been able to buy shares in the parent company, owned 100 per cent by Henry Ford. The new company acquired Ford's nine companies in continental Europe, paying its US parent £2.8 million for them.

Work soon began on the new Dagenham factory, where the ground-breaking ceremony took place on 16 May 1929 when Edsel Ford (standing in for his friend the Prince of Wales) cut the first sod with a silver spade. The spade hit a stone and bent, and had to be hammered straight on a railway line before the ceremony could proceed.

Watching the ceremony with interest was Edsel's eldest son, 11-year-old Henry Ford II, a round-faced boy in knickerbockers and cap, looking a trifle uneasy among the crowd of civic dignitaries. He was photographed with his father and Sir Percival Perry perched self-consciously on top of the first concrete pile to be driven home on the site. Afterwards, the Ford family toured the châteaux of the Loire in a Lincoln limousine – Lincoln had been Ford's luxury line since 1922, its gorgeous styling developed under Edsel's personal supervision – and young Henry kept a diary and drew maps of the entire journey. He pasted it all into a leather-bound album when he returned to Dearborn, and wrote captions beneath the pictures of the châteaux in his neat schoolboy hand.

Even though Dagenham represented the fulfilment of Perry's long-held view that Ford should replace Trafford Park with a brand-new factory that would be a credit to the British motor industry, Perry was unhappy with the location, and based his own offices in the West End of London, opposite the new Ford showroom at 88 Regent Street, which he had opened with a golden key in 1930. Doubtless still smarting over the loss of his Southampton site, he described Dagenham as 'almost the worst possible choice, whether from the standpoint of manufacture or that of marketing'.

The terrain was notoriously marshy, partly occupied by rubbish tips where London's waste was dumped or burned (one rat-ridden area was deep in rancid fat from London's meat markets), and partly by rough grazing where the local children used to play. A 40-acre lake known as the Breach recalled

The site was stabilised by sinking some 22,000 concrete piles to a depth of 80ft using massive steam hammers.

Concrete rafts were laid across the top of the piles to carry the factory. The space formed beneath the floor was used for storage and servicing the electric motors driving the factory machinery.

Laying the foundations for the blast furnace. Though work started on this site in 1930, it was not completed until 1934, when 'Cast Iron Charlie' Sorensen formally 'blew in' the furnace.

October 1930 and Henry Ford pays his first and last visit to the Dagenham factory, accompanied by Sir Percival Perry. A fleet of Lincolns and a lone Armstrong-Siddeley brought the motor magnate's party to the part-completed works.

The jetty was already in service by October 1931, but the anticipated volume of exports never materialised.

the floods that regularly inundated the site until it was controlled by drainage work in the 18th century. Further east were old London plague pits. Here, too, many tons of spoil excavated during the construction of the London Underground had been dumped. The Ford site was bounded on the east by Frog Island, a flat area that took its name from the fact that French prisoners of war had been confined there in Napoleonic times.

The architects of the new plant were Sir Charles Heathcote & Sons, with Sir Cyril Kirkpatrick as consulting engineer. Despite the shortcomings of the site, chosen as much for the publicity value of its proximity to London as for the ease with which ships could link it with major European ports, they planned the most ambitious factory construction ever undertaken by a European manufacturer. Covering an area of 66 acres, its buildings followed a general layout drawn up by Henry Ford's right-hand man 'Cast Iron Charlie' Sorensen.

The site was levelled by the big contracting company G. Percy Trentham, which moved tens of thousands of tons of earth in a matter of weeks and built ten miles of roads as well as railway tracks and bridges. Among the relics discovered when the site was cleared was an ancient wrought iron ship's anchor, buried 31ft below the current shore level. It had apparently been part of the equipment of a derelict ship used in around 1620 to close a breach in the river wall.

Before the factory could be erected, the site had to be stabilised by sinking around 22,000 concrete piles, cast in the adjoining Dagenham Dock site of the Samuel Williams shipping company. Already, the Dagenham statistics were impressive: laid end to end, the concrete piles would have covered a distance of some 170 miles. Massive steam hammers were used to drive them in, some to a depth of 80ft, and the factory was erected on concrete rafts laid on top of the piles.

Some 17,000 tons of steel were needed to make the framing and roof trusses of

Some 17,000 tons of steel were used to make the stanchions and trusses of the new factory's manufacturing and assembly shops. Ford's stand at the 1930 Schoolboys' Exhibition at Olympia was built in the shape of one of these buildings and housed an impressive model of the new factory.

The commercial vehicle version of the Ford Model A was the mainstay of Trafford Park and Dagenham production in the dark days of the Depression, when motorists bought smaller, less highly taxed cars.

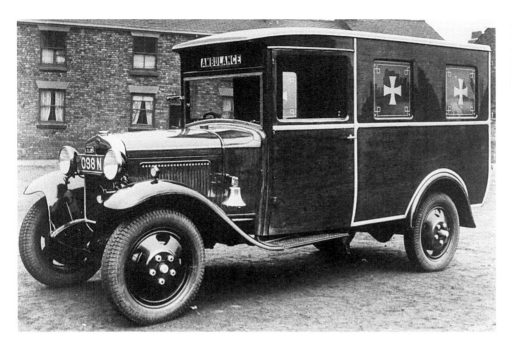

An ambulance version of the Model A, built by specialist manufacturers Herbert Lomas of Wilmslow, Cheshire.

the two main buildings, the Manufacturing and Assembly Shops. Nine million wood blocks were laid to form the floors and 16 acres of plate glass were used in the factory roofs. Storm gutters between the peaked roof sections were wide enough to take a car and capable of coping with the fiercest downpour the British climate could throw at them.

The new Dagenham works included its own power station, foundry, coke ovens and gas plants, plus the largest private wharf on the Thames, with an 1,800ft jetty capable of accommodating cargo ships with a capacity of 12,000 tons. Far in advance of his time, Henry Ford was a keen recycler, and he decreed that the Dagenham power station should burn London's rubbish, which was being dumped near his factory by the London County Council. This it was to do at the rate of 2,000 tons a week until 1939. Rumour has it that that Ford gave up the scheme when the LCC had the temerity to demand payment for its rubbish.

In the 1920s, Henry Ford was moving to conquer the air as well as the highways, with a subsidiary company, the Stout Metal Airplane Company, building the famous Ford Tri-Motor in Dearborn. When Henry Ford came to Britain in the spring of 1928 he met Sir Philip Sassoon, Under-Secretary of State for Air in the Government, who later that year visited Detroit. Perhaps encouraged by the visit, Henry Ford decided to sell the Tri-Motor in Europe, and naturally chose Ford-Britain to spearhead the venture.

A Tri-Motor was exhibited at the Olympia Aviation Show that summer, and proved a great success. The Duke of York (later King George VI) was apparently much impressed by it, while his brothers, the Prince of Wales and the Duke of Kent, flew in another Tri-Motor and declared themselves 'enchanted by their splendid – but too short – flight'.

After the Olympia exhibition closed, the show Tri-Motor set out on a

This attractive Braidwood-bodied fire engine was based on a Dagenham-built Ford Model AA truck chassis.

demonstration flight round Europe; by the time the trip ended in Prague in November, the Tri-Motor had visited 18 countries including Russia, made 325 flights and carried 3,750 passengers.

The Tri-Motor was sold to the Czech state airline and replaced late in 1930 by two demonstrator aircraft, one registered G-ABEF, for 'Edsel Ford') and the other G-ABHF (for 'Henry Ford'); these must have been among the first 'personalised' registrations on the British register.

Shortly before it was shipped to Europe, 'HF' set a new world 100km speed record of 164.432mph, beating the existing record by over 22mph. Before arriving in England, the two planes were sent on a whirlwind tour of Europe, visiting Milan, Athens and Belgrade.

On arrival in England, 'EF' and 'HF' were temporarily based at Heston, while a search was conducted for a permanent 'European Central Aircraft Assembly Plant'. Fortuitously, a suitable landing ground was located at Ford in Sussex, though sales were handled through Ford's Aviation Department, initially based in Perry's Regent Street office, then at Dagenham.

A number of Tri-Motors were sold in Europe, but the bold venture – which had done much to further the cause of civil aviation in America, where Tri-Motors operated the first transcontinental airliner services – failed to achieve the same level of success in Europe, and Ford's aviation factory would be closed in 1932 as a result of the downturn in sales caused by the depression.

Now that Henry Ford's master plan was in place, Perry set off to visit all Ford's European factories during 1929, accompanied by young Maurice Buckmaster, who had recently left Eton. Buckmaster was bilingual in French and also spoke German and Spanish, and had been hired by Perry to help coordinate Ford's European operations. "I joined Ford on Victoria Station," he recalled nearly 60 years later, "and Perry, his wife, valet and I left for Paris on the Golden Arrow."

In those days, Ford France was run by a Norwegian, Alexander Lie, who was not up to the job and was quickly sacked: four general managers followed in quick succession until in the early 1930s Buckmaster was installed as manager under the redoubtable Maurice Dollfus, a strong-willed former director of Hispano-Suiza.

Perry began appointing European directors to oversee the expansion of Ford's manufacturing empire across Europe. New factories were to assemble cars and trucks from kits of parts supplied by Dagenham. This bold plan would never be fully realised because of the rise of nationalism during the 1930s, when governments insisted on local manufacture of components, particularly in Germany, but also in France.

In Italy Ford's expansion plans – which included the take-over of the Isotta-Fraschini luxury car company – were thwarted by Mussolini, who owed a big favour to Giovanni Agnelli of Fiat, who had funded his rise to power.

To avoid Ford-Britain paying double income tax on the profits of the European companies, Perry set up a holding company, first in Liechtenstein, then in Luxembourg – and during the war in German-occupied Guernsey, with a branch office in London! The principal director of this 'Société des Investissements Ford', a pernickety Belgian named Camille Gutt, later became head of the International Monetary Fund.

Work on the Dagenham plant proceeded rapidly during 1929–30. In October 1930 Henry Ford, returning home via Essex after attending the Oberammergau Passion Play, paid his first and last visit to the part-completed factory. As he looked out of the window as his train rattled across the Essex countryside from Harwich to London, Ford was struck by the depressed state of the Essex farms. When Perry told him that British agriculture was in decline, Ford conceived the Co-Partnership Farms

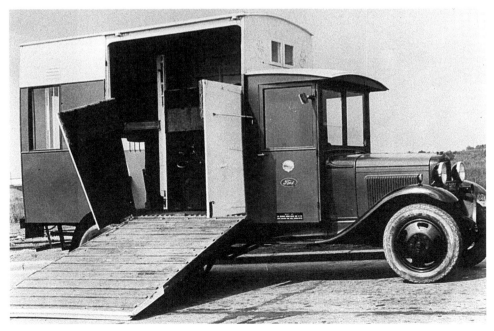

The Ford AA was a popular base for horse-boxes. Even the Prince of Wales owned one, built on a specially-converted six-wheeled chassis by Vincents of Reading.

Most expensive of the 1931
range was the Model A Fordor
saloon, an attractive proposition
at £225, but sales were negligible
as a result of the Depression.

venture on 2,000 acres of land bought from Lord Kenyon at Boreham to revitalise agriculture in the county.

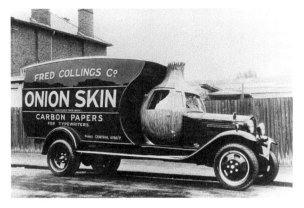

Interviewed by the press at Claridge's, Ford declared that 15 acres of buildings had already been completed at Dagenham, although the factory was still a year away from the start of production.

He remarked that as it had been found impossible to buy sufficient pig iron of the right quality from British suppliers, his company would build its own blast furnace.

Despite the worldwide depression, Ford refused to modify his plans, even when Perry told him of the delays in completing the power house and the rising costs of work on the Dagenham factory. Stepping nimbly across a makeshift plank bridge linking the shore to the jetty, the 68-year-old motor magnate joked with workmen as they cleaned red oxide rustproof paint off his overcoat with turpentine and cotton waste. Then he left to look at work on factory sites in Europe.

Maurice Buckmaster was sitting beside Henry Ford when the motor magnate visited a new plant that was being built in Rotterdam on a site chosen by Perry. 'Where's the water?' queried Ford, who insisted on deep-water berthing for freight vessels alongside his production plants, as his chauffeur-driven Lincoln rolled on to the factory site.

'A mile away, Mr Ford,' replied Buckmaster.

'No water, no plant!' snapped Henry. The Dutch officials looked on in stunned disbelief as Ford ordered his chauffeur to drive on. The Rotterdam plant was abandoned in favour of a new site beside a ship canal at Amsterdam...

Perry's experience with the Slough Trading Estate led him to plan a similar industrial estate at Dagenham, and further parcels of land were acquired which brought the site area to around 600 acres by 1932. However, the only companies which actually set up factories there were all Ford suppliers, such as Briggs Motor Bodies – which had previously shipped body panels to Ford-Britain from its plant in Detroit for assembly at Trafford Park – and the Kelsey-Hayes Wheel Company. These would eventually be absorbed by Ford as it sought greater control over production.

To the north of the factory, the London County Council was building a vast council estate around the ancient village of Dagenham to rehouse East End families displaced by slum clearance. This looked like a reason for Ford's choice of the Dagenham site, but it was in fact coincidental, and much of the Dagenham workforce would come from outside the area.

As the Dagenham plant neared completion, the sales of Ford's private cars – treated by Britain's foolish horsepower tax as though they were large luxury cars despite their modest first cost – suffered a catastrophic slump as Depression-hit customers shifted their allegiance to smaller-engined economy models like the Austin

End of an era. The last vehicle to leave the Trafford Park production line was this Model A van. The production machinery was already on its way south to Dagenham.

Seven and Morris Eight. Oddly enough, Ford sold the smaller-engined 2043cc 14.9hp model for £5 more than the 3285cc 24hp version, 'to encourage (said Henry Ford) the motoring public to use the more efficient car'.

The cost of building the plant was running seriously over budget, and the strain on Ford's resources was immense. One curious 'economy' was the purchase of a second-hand direct current convertor from the San Francisco Cable Car Company to power the DC motors of the quayside cranes. Nevertheless, the company maintained its momentum.

The only modification to the master plan was the abandonment of a scheme to continue spare-part production in the old factory at Trafford Park, which was instead closed in December 1931 and sold. Now everything was concentrated at Dagenham and the changeover of production during the autumn of 1931 was made as seamless as possible by moving the machinery and key workers at weekends. Railway sidings ran straight into the factory so that machines could be unloaded alongside ready-prepared mountings, slid into place on blocks of ice and bolted down ready to start running on the Tuesday morning after the move.

It didn't always work so well: some skilled toolmakers arrived at Dagenham to find that their machines were still in Manchester and were considerably annoyed to be told to sweep the floors for the time being.

Some 2,000 key workers and their furniture were brought down from Manchester by train, but that was as far as company welfare went. Once they got off the train at Dagenham, they were on their own when it came to finding somewhere to live. The discovery that rents were higher in the south came as a rude shock to many of them, and only a few months after the factory opened, the workers went on strike for three days. This resulted in the wages of the top grade being cut and the savings shared among the lower grades, for there were strict government limits on overall pay.

Perry, resentful of the strike, blamed a few hotheads among the workforce for embarrassing him at a difficult time for Dagenham, but directed his main anger at the Government, accusing it of bleeding the motor industry dry. Despite the loss of £682,000 recorded by Ford-Britain in 1932, the company still had to pay £44,000 in tax. Coming on top of the £217,000 tax bill imposed the previous year, which turned a profit of £83,000 into a loss of £134,000, his anger was justified. But motoring, as ever, was a convenient milch cow for the Treasury, which, to compensate for falling revenues from the horsepower tax as Depression-hit motorists turned away from cars like the Model A, which had relatively large engines, in favour of smaller-engined economy models, raised petrol tax to 50 per cent.

It was not a happy prospect for Dagenham.

Chapter Three

A LIGHTHOUSE
OF HOPE

THE new factory was hailed by the press as 'an example of heroic pluck, this hive of industry which stands like a lighthouse of hope in a storm-tossed sea of industry'. It certainly boasted every modern convenience: the buildings had devices that filtered the air and extracted the dust, while the windows were opened and closed electronically. On-site medical facilities included a doctor and trained nurses, an operating theatre, X-ray equipment, a dispensary and first-aid stations. Eight canteens were strategically located throughout the factory so that no worker had to walk for more than two minutes to reach one. Ford spoke bravely of a potential output of 1,000–1,500 vehicles a day from Dagenham, but the economic climate was far from favourable.

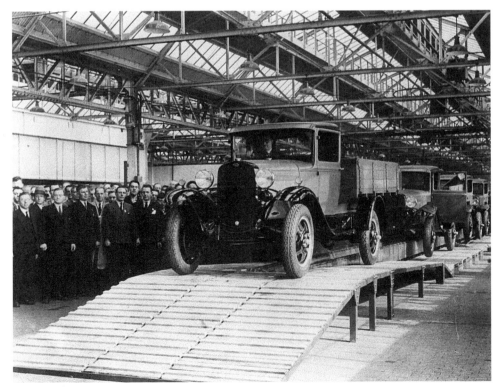

Works manager Rowland Smith drives Dagenham's first vehicle, 30-cwt truck AA4791110, off the production line on 1 October 1931. Fifty years later he would ceremonially repeat the drive-away as passenger in an identical truck during Dagenham's 50th anniversary celebrations.

Detroit-on-Thames takes a bow – a biplane's-eye-view of the Dagenham plant, still surrounded by fields. The 'Ford' sign was added to the powerhouse in 1936: almost 170ft long and 60ft high, it was one of the largest neon signs ever made, and was visible for several miles.

There was pride but only partial cause for celebration when Rowland Smith drove the first vehicle – a Model AA truck – off the production line at Dagenham on 1 October 1931. The choice of a commercial vehicle was significant: with the country in the grip of depression, Ford's private car sales had declined almost to vanishing point, and it was truck sales that kept the plant running. In the first quarter of production, Dagenham turned out 4,569 trucks and sold just five cars. Indeed, the drastic fall-off in the sale of cars made Ford in Detroit ponder whether to cut its losses and close down Ford-Britain as a manufacturing centre.

The year 1932 saw the introduction of Ford's immortal V8. This is the original 1932 Model 18, photographed by Ford in front of London's Admiralty Arch.

Perry was at least partially to blame for this disastrous start, for the years he had spent living in the tiny Channel Island of Herm, where cars were forbidden – at 300 acres, it was smaller than the new Dagenham plant – had left him out of touch. He opposed the production of small cars, as there was little profit in them. On the other hand, Henry Ford realised that there was a significant market for small-engined cars in Europe and ordered a shipment of representative British economy cars to be sent to Detroit in 1928. More followed at the end of 1930, when Ford's office thanked the British company for a Humber tourer and 'the three cases of small cars'. When Henry Ford showed Perry designs for a

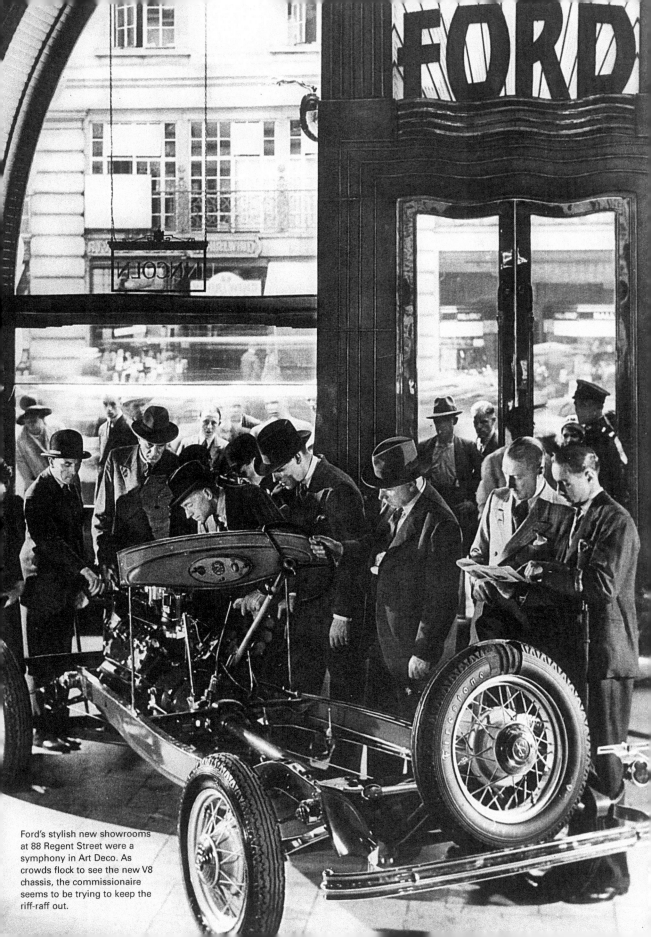

Ford's stylish new showrooms at 88 Regent Street were a symphony in Art Deco. As crowds flock to see the new V8 chassis, the commissionaire seems to be trying to keep the riff-raff out.

new small car, the Englishman was unenthusiastic. But as British Ford sales plummeted alarmingly, Perry was forced into a U-turn and in desperation he appealed to Henry Ford to produce a miracle small car to save the British firm from bankruptcy.

The Detroit giant swung into action in October 1931, when its chief engineer, Laurence Sheldrick, sketched out a simple 8hp car with a 933cc four-cylinder sidevalve engine built in unit with a three-speed gearbox. The little car only represented a marginal advance over the old Model T in its chassis layout, which had single transverse leaf springs fore and aft.

Code-named 'Model 19' (the famed Ford V8, which was also under development at that time was 'Model 18'), the new car stood apart from its contemporaries by virtue of its ultra-modern body styling. This was the work of former yacht designer Eugene Turenne 'Bob' Gregorie, recruited by Edsel Ford to bring a smart new look

In 1933 Scotland Yard took delivery of these new 14.9hp Model BF Ford saloons for the Flying Squad. They also acquired a cutaway Model B chassis to instruct students at the Hendon Police College in modern engineering practice – and used it for over 40 years.

to Ford products. He was one of the first body designers to model prototype bodies in clay, and his invention of the 'measuring bridge', a mobile template from which precise measurements could be taken from the clay model to create accurate dimensional drawings and body tooling changed body design from an imperfect art into a fundamental part of the production process.

Intriguingly, an early 'clay' of the new car featured headlamps incorporated into the front wings, an advanced design concept that was a trademark feature of America's exclusive Pierce-Arrow marque.

Ford-Britain's general manager Rowland Smith, whose experience with Standard gave him a far better grasp of what the public wanted from a small family car than his chairman, headed a small team of Dagenham staff sent over to Dearborn.

'I carried an envelope in either inside pocket,' he recalled many years later. 'When I met Henry Ford, I handed him the envelope from my left pocket, which contained

One of Ford's company Tri-Motors at Ford Aerodrome in Sussex. The grass was cropped by the Ford pedigree herd of sheep, 'famous all over the world', though they must have posed a problem for landing aircraft!

Registered G-ABHF (for 'Henry Ford'), this Model 5-AT-C Tri-Motor was sold to New Guinea in 1934 and, after flying service in the gold fields, crashed over a 100ft cliff in 1941 and was written off.

the specification of the car we needed for Britain. He looked at the contents and nodded: "We'll see what we can do," he said. It was just as well; the envelope in my right pocket contained my resignation!'

Smith and his men helped with the development of the new model, which was, recalled Sheldrick, 'done pretty darn quick'. Even the 68-year-old Henry Ford lent a hand in the work, which went on through holidays and weekends, and even over Christmas.

As early as mid-January 1932, rumours began to circulate that Dagenham was planning something revolutionary to respond to the economic crisis: when Ernest Appleby of *Autocar* magazine encountered Sir Percival Perry dining with a friend in the exclusive Hungaria Restaurant in Lower Regent Street, he realised something was afoot.

A few days later *Autocar* had its scoop, publishing a double-page spread entitled 'A Ford small car for British market' featuring artists' impressions of the new baby car and a photograph which was obviously a sneak picture of the Dearborn clay model. It must have been leaked to the magazine by one of Smith's team.

The official launch of the new car took place at the Ford Exhibition at London's Albert Hall on Friday 19 February. Many years before, the British Ford company had fallen out with the Society of Motor Manufacturers & Traders, the representative body of the British motor industry, and since the mid-1920s had organised its own 'fringe' show at the same time as the SMMT's annual Motor Show at Olympia.

Beneath a splendid transparent Art Deco arch, septuagenarian A.E. Rumsey, Britain's oldest Ford dealer principal, pulled a sheet off the new Ford 'baby' and a crowd of dealers surged forward to admire it. The new 'Model Y' had gone from drawing board to finished prototype in five months: modern manufacturers may take two or three years to reach the same point.

Initially, it had been hoped that the first of the new 8hp Ford cars would leave the production line at Dagenham during May, but the Albert Hall Show – and similar exhibitions held simultaneously across Europe, thanks to the existence of 14 Model Y prototypes shipped over from Dearborn – gave Ford officials the chance to quiz dealers and the public about the design features of the new car.

As a result of this first-ever 'customer clinic', the car which went into production in Dagenham in August 1932 differed in many respects from the prototype. The radiator shell was more modern in appearance, the body was wider, the petrol tank

was at the rear of the car instead of under the bonnet and the engine had been revised.

Bob Gregorie's 'new look' Model Y was particularly striking, with a heart-shaped radiator grille gently curving forward into the valance between the flared front wings, and Edsel Ford asked him to scale up the design for the 1933 Model 40 V8.

The 10 months it had taken to go from drawing board to full production of the Model Y was a remarkable achievement, but Ford had spent some £5 million on the Dagenham works and there had been little chance of recouping any of this on the flagging sales of the Model A. Happily, the Model Y – the most modern-looking small car on the British market – saved the day. It had remarkably few teething troubles, apart from some frustrating problems with the rear axle, solved by a hasty redesign while dealers in hilly areas kept their customers on the road by 'borrowing' crownwheel and pinion sets from unsold cars.

Though Ford recorded only small profits in 1931–32 and went £160,249 into the red in 1932–33, the following year a profit of £1.39 million was recorded. During 1933 Ford-Britain built nearly 33,000 Model Ys, giving Dagenham nearly 19 per cent of the British market and making it number three in the sales league. The company was back in profit and in 1934 the Model Y gave Ford 54 per cent of the British market for cars of 8hp and under, against such formidable rivals as the Austin Seven and the Morris Eight, which shamelessly aped the little Ford's distinctive

Ford has run factory tours in its British plants since 1914. In the 1930s, over 60,000 visitors a year toured the plant. Here Rowland Smith *(centre)* accompanies a VIP tour of Dagenham conducted by a factory guide in peaked cap and white dustcoat.

The British-built Model B Ford differed in minor respects from its American counterpart. This 1932 Fordor bodied by Briggs of Dagenham has rear-hinged 'suicide doors' all round – American Model Bs had forward hinges on their front doors.

styling while adding hydraulic brakes instead of Ford's mechanical units. Singer, too, introduced a Model Y look-alike called the Bantam.

In June 1932 Perry had signed an agreement with Ford-Canada 'to ensure that the supply of Ford cars throughout the Empire shall be derived from an Empire factory'. This resulted in the Model Y being assembled by the local companies in Australia and New Zealand, while V8s for Britain (and the European companies under its control) would be supplied by Ford-Canada.

Additionally, Ford's European factories in Cologne, Paris, Cork, Copenhagen and Barcelona all assembled the Model Y, though it was never as popular in those markets as in its native Britain. Dagenham's role as the common supply source for Europe was quickly usurped by the economic conditions of the times. It was only a couple of years before Ford-Germany was forced to buy all the parts it could not make itself from suppliers within the borders of Hitler's Third Reich in order that it could be recognised as a German company. The situation deteriorated to the point that Ford-America effectively re-acquired the German and French companies in 1934. Dagenham had to swallow a loss of 3 million reichsmarks on the German deal.

Mussolini's Italy, keen to keep the

The Model Y was assembled from Dagenham-made components in Ford-Iberia's plant in Barcelona until the Spanish Civil War brought an end to production.

The 8-hp model Y was launched in prototype form at a special Ford exhibition in the White City at the beginning of 1932. After analysing criticisms from dealers and customers, the design was heavily modified before production began in August 1932.

market clear for Fiat, imposed ridiculously high tariffs on imported cars. The little Model Y stood no hope of selling there except as a novelty for the rich, as an import duty of £184 was levied, bringing the showroom price to £364 (in Britain it sold for just £120). In 1934 the tax was increased to £282.

In Ireland the Depression hit Cork badly, with only 19 Ford cars registered in the first six months of 1932, compared to 1,012 the previous year. The plant's woes were compounded by the introduction of high duties on imported vehicles and components after the election of February 1932, which sparked off a trade war between Britain and the Irish Free State. It was a fatal blow for the Cork foundry, which had been trying to keep its head above the financial waters by producing lavatory cisterns, gutters and drainpipes. Ford-Britain, which had taken over Cork in 1928, bypassed the Irish tariffs by simply transferring both foundry and tractor production to Dagenham within a matter of months, along with a considerable number of workers from the Cork factory.

The production process at Dagenham in the 1930s was as near self-contained as any car factory would ever be in the history of the British motor industry. Ford's jetty was equipped with two impressively-titled 'Electric Crank-operating Horizontal Luffing Gantry Cranes', running on rails with a 17ft gauge and big enough to straddle a goods train. These could lift loads of up to five tons from ships berthed alongside the jetty.

Mounted on the 'High Line' – the upper deck of the jetty – were Europe's largest unloading cranes, which gulped iron ore and limestone for the blast furnace (symbolically 'blown in' on completion in 1934 by 'Cast Iron Charlie' Sorensen) and coal for the coke ovens in bites of six tons at a time from the holds of ships. The raw

Former Aston Martin mechanic Jack Bezzant marketed this neat supercharged sports version of the 8hp Model Y in 1933. Here he is in the passenger seat in Bournemouth at the end of the 1934 RAC Rally, in which his car came joint ninth in its class.

Sir Percival Perry *(front row, centre)* with what is believed to be a group of foreign dealers, sometime in the early 1930s.

materials were dropped into hoppers which automatically weighed them and, once a full load was recorded, discharged them into electric transfer cars with a capacity of 50 tons. These ran along the 'High Line' beneath the unloaders and tipped the raw material into a store yard which could hold 130,000 tons.

The coal was taken to be pulverised, screened and delivered to the ovens to be

converted into coke for the blast furnace and foundry, while a bridge crane loaded the iron ore into 'weighing cars', feeding the blast furnace and foundry.

Nothing was wasted: the gases produced in the process of turning coal into coke were stored in a 2 million cu ft gas-holder and then converted into tar, ammonia sulphate and benzole in the By-Products Plant. Ore dust created by the smelting of the iron was, claimed Ford, filtered out to be used to make clinker to fuel the blast furnace, though employees recall that enough escaped to create considerable fall-out throughout the site, and staff were given a six-monthly allowance of oxalic acid to clean the dust off their cars. The foundry provided all the iron needed to make Dagenham's castings in lots of 75 tons at a time, while Dagenham's rolling mills spewed out 45 tons of steel bars and 30 tons of steel strip in every eight-hour shift.

Iron was cast into pigs – small bars which would be later melted in the foundry to make castings – or tipped into mixers for immediate use. The special sand used to make the casting moulds was continuously cleaned and recycled as the moulds were broken to reveal the red-hot castings.

Five miles of monorail conveyor linked the foundry and the machine shop, while an intricate network of conveyors criss-crossed the entire factory, carrying parts and

Ford, which many years before had broken with the Society of Motor Manufacturers & Traders, organised its own motor show in the Albert Hall as a rival attraction to the SMMT's official Olympia Exhibition. This is the 1935 Ford Show, with the sensational £100 Ford Popular the focus of attention.

'By river to Britain's Wonder Factory' – during the 1930s, Ford ran a fast powerboat service between London and Dagenham and also used 150-passenger steamers to bring the public from Westminster Pier to Dagenham at a return fare of 3s 6d so that they could tour the factory.

In October 1935 Ford's ruthless cost-cutting brought the price of the Model Y down to £100, the first and only time a mass-produced four-seater saloon had ever been sold at such a price. It enabled many families to afford their first new car.

It can be yours –

THE £100 FORD SALOON

sub-assemblies to the precise point in the production process where they were needed. In dramatic contrast with the average factory, with its overhead shafting and belts, Dagenham used individual electric motors to drive the production machinery. Some 5,000 motors had been ordered from the old-established electrical company Crompton Parkinson; it was the biggest-ever single order of its kind.

In the factory's machine shops, metal components passed through a series of machines, each one set to perform one particular operation, until they were ready to be taken to the assembly shop. At each stage machined components were inspected and compared with incredibly precise gauges – Ford produced the industry standard Johannson Gauge Blocks, accurate to two-millionths of an inch – to ensure complete standardisation: any component that failed the tests was either scrapped or remade.

For example, the rough crankshaft forgings underwent 18 separate machining operations in 16 minutes, while connecting rods were subjected to 54 separate operations, each one measured to an accuracy of one-thousandth of an inch.

While this was going on, the gauges themselves were also subject to regular testing to ensure that they still complied with the master standards.

The huge quantities of materials entering and leaving the factory were carried by high-speed overhead cranes capable of travelling at up to 500 feet per minute: these were made by the distinguished electrical company Royce Ltd, founded by engineer Henry Royce, who had been born in the same year (1863) as Henry Ford and achieved fame for teaming up with the Hon Charles Rolls in 1904 to make superlative motor cars.

Curiously, one crucial component not manufactured at Dagenham in the 1930s was the chassis frame for the larger Ford cars and trucks, the pressings for which were produced in Shropshire by Joseph Sankey, a company which had been supplying Ford since 1919.

This was very much the exception to the Ford rule. Even though the Kelsey-Hayes

The new 10hp Model C and the Model Y come off the same assembly line at Dagenham in 1934. Evident are the light-coloured Electric Blue Model Ys, a colour option available only during the 1934 season.

Dagenham only started building the V8 in March 1935: before that, V8 models had been imported from Ford-Canada. In November 1935 Ford launched the V8-68, which proved to be the best-selling 3.6-litre Ford V8 of the 1930s, with sales totalling 4,527 in just over 13 months.

and Briggs plants at Dagenham were independently owned and in theory could take work from any car company, in effect they were an extension of the Ford production process. The Kelsey-Hayes welded wire wheels were for some years an essential feature of Ford cars in the period when wood-spoked wheels were replaced by all-metal wheels. The production process was unique, based on a special jig shaped like a big plate with a hollow centre and grooves arranged precisely to position the spokes in relation to the finished hub and rim. Once the spokes were laid in the jig, they were electrically welded in sequence, the whole job taking only a few minutes before the wheel was ready for final cleaning and enamelling.

Later, pressed steel wheels were adopted and these could be produced at the rate of 30,000 a week. Kelsey-Hayes also made hubs and brake drums for Dagenham.

The Briggs Body Works, with a staff of some 4,000, produced all the coachwork for Dagenham and – initially – its European satellite plants. In the early 1930s, Ford bodies used ash frames built up in jigs to which steel panels were attached. It was claimed that a saloon could be completely rolled over without the body collapsing. Later, all-steel welded construction was adopted.

The body pressings were relatively small, welded together in jig tools that cost £5,000 and located the panels by pneumatic pressure. It was claimed that this method of construction resulted in a stronger body than if larger sheets were used, but it meant that until after World War Two Briggs lacked the capacity to stamp out metal roof panels. Therefore, Ford saloons of the period had fabric-covered roofs which were difficult to repair if they leaked, although they did eliminate the annoying drumming that was a feature of many early closed metal bodies.

Although windows were fitted on the Ford assembly lines – the company used some 14 acres of safety glass a year – and seats were trimmed in the Ford upholstery shops, the bodies were otherwise supplied to Ford ready trimmed and painted; export bodies were shipped untrimmed. Even so, the Briggs works consumed around 110 miles of upholstery a year.

Patrick Hennessy was a star in the ascendant during the 1930s. He revolutionised Ford's purchasing procedures and struck up a friendship with the Ford family which endured until his death in the 1980s.

In the 1930s Briggs, which literally depended on Ford for its very existence and had a sales manager whose main task was liaising with the neighbouring Ford plant, had an unconventionally liberal idea of 'customer relations'. Some years ago a retired senior Ford manager told me of the parties held by the head of Briggs at Dagenham to entertain his Ford clients. On arriving at his house in Upminster, a highly respectable dormitory town for Dagenham management, the Ford men were welcomed at the door by attractive young ladies carrying drinks and wearing little more than a broad smile!

During his visit to Dagenham on 13 July 1934 the Prince of Wales was shown round the Ford Trade School, which gave promising youngsters a start in life by teaching them mechanical engineering skills. It even provided one future chairman of Ford-Britain, for (Sir) William Batty was a former Trade School boy.

The most popular of all Dagenham's 1930s V8 models, the 1936 22hp Model 62, had a 2.2-litre engine originally designed for Matford, a Strasbourg-based joint venture between Ford and the French Mathis company. The body, too, was identical to the French car, though it was built at Dagenham by Briggs.

Ford's 'in-house' foundry was proving a valuable asset, and in July 1935 Dagenham began making the cylinder blocks for the V8 model that had previously been imported from Canada. Perry had responded to a call from Henry Ford for increased output of V8 engines, which were fitted to all Dagenham-built heavy trucks.

Perry hoped that Dagenham-built V8 cars might restore some of his lost export business, but this was not to be. On the home market, sales of the highly-taxed 3.6-litre V8 were never great and Perry complained to the Government that he could have sold many more of these stylish cars under a fairer road tax regime. The launch in 1935 of a smaller V8 powered by the 2.2-litre 'Alsace' engine, originally designed for the French 'Matford', saw a modest increase in V8 sales.

Both sizes of V8 were used in Dagenham's comprehensive truck range. This proved a mixed blessing, for although the V8 gave a usefully large power output, it was also thirsty and attracted higher taxation, so from 1937 a less costly four-cylinder power unit option became available for Ford commercials.

Ford's small car range was augmented by a van version of the Model Y and a curious three-wheeled 'mechanical horse' – also based on the Model Y – called the Tug, but only around 120 examples of the latter were sold.

Under severe pressure from its rivals, Ford embarked on a course of ruthless cost-cutting which brought the price of the Model Y down from £120 to £115 in

The first Ford to have a model name, the 1939 10hp Prefect got its name because it was 'at the head of its class'.

December 1934, from £115 to £110 in September 1935 and finally – with dealer profit margins now purely nominal – from £110 to £100 in October 1935. No mass-produced four-seater saloon had ever been sold at such a price (nor ever would again), but the gamble paid off: the pared-to-the-bone 'Popular' doubled Ford's share of the 8hp sector and the company never looked back.

Dearborn had already developed the Model Y theme a stage further with the 1172cc 10hp Model C-20 of 1934, whose sidevalve power unit was to be the backbone of Ford's family car range until the end of the 1950s. The 'Model C' added a small four-door saloon to the range (the Model Y was only built as a two-door saloon) and a tourer became available in May 1935. A letter to Perry from Henry Ford's right-hand man, the Danish-born 'Cast Iron Charlie' Sorensen, reveals that Dearborn planned a tiny V8 version of this car which never made production.

Sorensen, incidentally, attempted to export the grim working practices which he had favoured in Dearborn to Dagenham, keeping workers 'on their toes' by sending over teams of 'inspectors' who would go through the offices dismissing employees that they thought were not pulling their weight on the spot. This earned them the unflattering nickname of 'Yougos', from the random way that they would tell someone: 'You go!' Fifty years later a long-term employee recalled that 'once the Yougos had gone, the chaps they had dismissed were usually taken back.'

The second half of the 1930s saw significant expansion of the Dagenham facilities. The great expenditure on the power-house, blast furnace and coke ovens was showing a

Visiting England in the late 1930s, Edsel Ford takes time off to stay on the farm of a British friend.

Ford's small cars had their commercial equivalents, and Ford's publicity department proposed this stylishly-lettered 'design for a butcher' to prospective purchasers of the 8hp E04C 5cwt van. Sadly, this new model was planned for the 1940 season.

The daringly streamlined body of the 1937 3.6-litre Ford V8-78 was inspired by the avant-garde styling of its costlier cousin the Lincoln Zephyr.

good return, quite apart from the vital service they gave the factory. The power house – which carried a giant Ford sign 140ft by 60ft that could be seen from 20 miles away – generated enough electricity for a town of 180,000 inhabitants. Each year the blast furnace produced 200,000 tons of pig iron and the coke ovens made 400,000 gallons of benzole and 2.5 million gallons of coal tar. Outside customers had begun purchasing the electricity, pig-iron, coke, gas and by-products which were surplus to the factory's needs. The slag from the furnace, for instance, was converted

When Nazi Germany sent its new Arado 196 floatplane on a demonstration flight to Finland in 1938, this Dagenham-built Fordson industrial tractor was used to haul it ashore near the capital Helsingfors (Helsinki).

As well as welcoming the general public, Dagenham also laid on tours for VIP visitors. Here, a Dagenham official shows a party of Portuguese dignitaries the workings of the Dagenham jetty.

Vehicle Developments of Stratford Place in London's West End offered a range of special-bodied Fords commissioned from specialist coachbuilders. This 1938 eight-seat limousine on the V8-81A chassis was apparently built for them by Corsica of Cricklewood, better known for its one-off sports car bodywork.

into Tarmacadam by a local firm and used to resurface roads and footpaths in Greater London. New building work begun in 1936 included a doubling in size of the foundry and the construction of a rolling mill and spring-making section.

Factory tours had been part of Ford's public relations strategy since the early days of Trafford Park, and nearly 50,000 visitors a year came to see production at

In 1938 Briggs built a total of 62,137 passenger and commercial vehicles in its Dagenham works. This was already nearly three-and-a-half times the plant's planned capacity: by 1948 the figure had risen to around 90,000, and the plant really was bursting at the seams.

Dagenham, which had 15,000 employees by the end of the 1930s. The plant boasted a reception area for visitors displaying new cars and what was then Britain's oldest Ford, a 1907 Model N four-seater bought for £8 from a garage in Horley, Surrey, and a cinema showing Ford publicity films. Among the famous names in the company's visitors' book were aviatrix Amy Johnson, comedian Sir Harry Lauder and the Prince of Wales – Dagenham had to telegraph Dearborn for special permission to serve the royal visitor a whisky and soda after his tour, as Henry Ford had decreed that all his plants should be 'dry'. Henry Ford's son Edsel came to Dagenham with his teenaged sons Henry II and Benson in 1936.

Ford had always placed a great emphasis on after-sales service – indeed, Sir Percival Perry claimed to have been the first to use the word 'service' in connection with motor cars – and dealers were encouraged to bring their operations and equipment to a high level of efficiency. Dealer conferences were held regularly throughout Britain, refresher courses for dealership mechanics were organised at

A publicity shot of the V8-91A, the first Ford to feature hydraulic brakes (Henry Ford didn't trust them, believing that mechanical connections were safer). But what is the man in the foreground up to? Has she just knocked him down?

The 'Ford Gymkhana' at Brooklands was the most popular event ever organised at the Surrey racetrack, attracting a crowd of 30,000. Ford cars were demonstrated on the finishing straight, and there was a race on the Campbell circuit. The car parks were full to overflowing.

Among the attractions staged at the 1939 Ford Gymkhana was this display of stunt driving by Ford V8s, which knocked down barrels and drove through fire and plate glass.

The slogan at Brooklands was 'the right crowd and no crowding'. But there was certainly crowding at the Ford Gymkhana where 'the paddock and the old finishing straight, bedecked with signs and bunting, had assumed an unaccustomed air of gaiety'.

Dagenham and specially equipped vans visited every distributor to ensure that they knew their products thoroughly.

Perry continued to maintain his office in Regent Street as the nerve centre of Ford's European operations and in the mid-1930s recalled Maurice Buckmaster from Paris to assist him. Also employed in the Office of Sir Percival Perry was the mysterious 'Mr Orleans', who was actually a Spanish prince, the cousin of the deposed King Alfonso XIII.

In 1938, Perry became a peer as Lord Perry of Stock Harvard, taking his title from the picturesque Essex village where he lived. He presided over a board of directors which had been strengthened in 1937 by the addition of Britain's famous racing motorist, Sir Malcolm Campbell, making Ford-Britain the only motor company ever

to have two land speed record holders (Campbell and Henry Ford himself, who had reached 91.37 mph at the tiller of his 18.5-litre '999' in 1904) on its board.

At Campbell's suggestion, Ford would, in 1939, organise a 'Ford Gymkhana' at the Brooklands racetrack in Surrey, which turned out to be the most popular event ever organised there. Among the star exhibits was a midget racer, originally built for Edsel's youngest son William Clay Ford, which Old Henry had given Campbell in gratitude for lending his land speed record car *Blue Bird* to the Henry Ford Museum in Detroit (and to prevent young Billy Ford from breaking his neck

as, with schoolboy ingenuity, he had found a way of disconnecting the governor fitted to the car to restrict its speed).

Dagenham now wanted more independence and the bodywork for the 1937 versions of the 8 and 10hp models had been designed in Essex rather than Michigan. This, of course, was a total break with established Ford procedure and there was a degree of trepidation about getting official approval for these models. When it came

Personalised number plates are nothing new: this Anglia carries 'FMC 7', one of a series of 'FMC' indices acquired by Ford in the 1930s. The Anglia was launched after the outbreak of war in 1939, and only 5,136 were built before production ceased in 1941. When the model reappeared in 1945, it had no running boards.

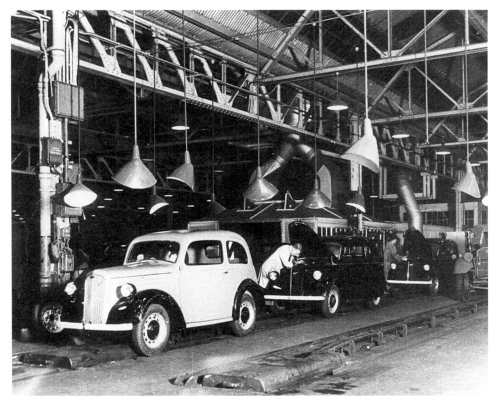

Painted white, the first 1940 Anglia leaves the production line. But already Dagenham is on a war footing and a military V8 truck is coming down the adjacent track.

to choosing a senior manager to accompany the prototypes to Dearborn, Patrick Hennessy drew the short straw, perhaps because he came from Cork like Henry Ford's father and might strike a chord with the motor billionaire, who prided himself on his Irish roots.

When Hennessy arrived in Dearborn, he was confronted by Charles Sorensen, who was visibly annoyed by the breach of protocol and told Hennessy to 'take an axe and chop up the prototypes'. He was only half joking!

Then Hennessy was summoned to the presence of Henry Ford himself. 'He was,' recalled Hennessy to the author 40 years later, 'the only man of whom I was ever frightened; he was so unpredictable.'

And Henry's reaction was typically unexpected. 'Do you like children, Hennessy?' he asked the young Irishman.

'Yes, Mr Ford, I have two of them,' replied Hennessy.

'Good,' said Ford. 'Let's go and play baseball!'

So the pair walked over to the Greenfield Village open-air museum, where Ford had established a schoolhouse on the green by the picturesque Martha-Mary Chapel. Old Henry told the children to take time out and Hennessy and the motor billionaire played baseball with them until panicky Ford executives came searching for their missing chief, anxious because he hadn't told anyone where he was going.

With Henry Ford's blessing, the new models were accepted and duly went into production. They led the way to the creation of two of the best-known British Ford lines, the 10hp Prefect of 1938 (the first Ford model in the world to have a name instead of a series letter) and the 8hp Anglia, announced shortly after the outbreak of war in October 1939.

A unique bond sprang up between Hennessy and the Ford family. Edsel Ford's sons Henry, Benson and William called the Irishman 'Uncle Pat' to the end of his days, even when Hennessy had become chairman of Ford-Britain and Henry Ford II was chief executive of Ford worldwide.

Industrial Unit Development

Inevitably, production of engines at Dagenham outstripped the output of cars, and Ford set up an Industrial Unit Department to cope with the demand. The applications seemed endless: specialist car makes like Morgan and Allard used Ford power, and the company's range of four-cylinder and V8 engines were used in cranes, boats, fire-pumps, railcars and a host of other applications. These are just a few of the dozens of uses that industry found for Ford engines.

John Allen Ltd of Oxford's elaborate ditcher and excavator.

D. Wickham's rail inspection car and gang trolley.

The Kronfeld Trainer taught pilots to fly without leaving the ground.

Sky Publicity's
searchlight projected
advertising messages
on to the clouds.

These Vickers-Armstrong 'Utility
Tractors' were the forerunner of the
wartime Bren gun carrier.

A marine conversion of the 24-hp
Model B engine.

V8 power for a railcar chassis.

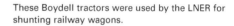

The Chaseside Hi-Lift mechanical shovel.

These Boydell tractors were used by the LNER for shunting railway wagons.

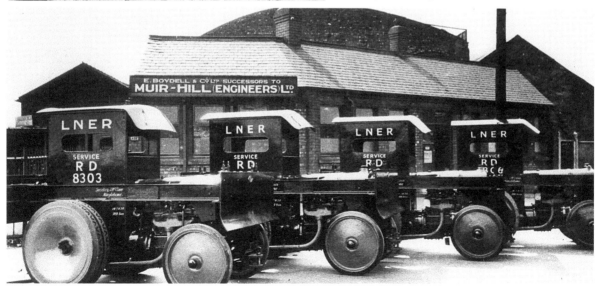

Chapter Four

'MOST EXCELLENT VEHICLES'

T HE outbreak of war on 3 September 1939 had little effect on Dagenham. It was that curious period of inertia that came to be known as the 'Phoney War' when 'England appeared to be marking time and to be unable or unwilling to key her industries to war-time pitch'.

For Ford, which had the capacity to build 120,000 vehicles and millions of spare parts a year, it was an intensely frustrating time. The only change in routine was the use of the jetty to evacuate some 17,000 local people – particularly nursing mothers and babies – aboard six paddle steamers. The factory continued to tick over at its peacetime working pattern of 40 hours a week and the only official instructions came in the form of advice on how to immobilise the factory in the event of an enemy invasion. Ford duly drew up an elaborate manual for departmental heads detailing the means of rendering the factory's stocks of petrol and benzole useless, immobilising completed vehicles and engines, dispersing spare parts, vital documents and drawings, damping down the blast furnace and putting the power house out of action.

Anyway, the government apparently thought that Dagenham, with its 'huge bulk along the north bank of the Thames, its chimneys capped with plumes of smoke, its blast furnace glowing at night like a ruby in an Ethiop's ear', would be a sitting target for the anticipated Luftwaffe air raids and only placed very small orders with Ford. The company was, despite its long history of building vehicles for Britain's roads, still regarded as something of an outsider by the national press and industry. So all the company was initially asked to produce were a few trucks for the Forestry Commission, the Ministry of Health and the Ministry of Home Security and an ongoing order from the Air Ministry for balloon winch trucks.

Only the Ministry of Agriculture & Fisheries showed confidence in Dagenham, and – following a suggestion by Ford that in the event of war the country would have a greatly increased need for tractors – early in 1939 ordered 3,000 tractors, to be stored in depots all over England to be immediately available for food production should war be declared. And to be bought back at cost price by Ford if it wasn't.

In fact, the stockpile of tractors proved invaluable, for when war broke out 3 million extra acres of land were ploughed up for food production, and the

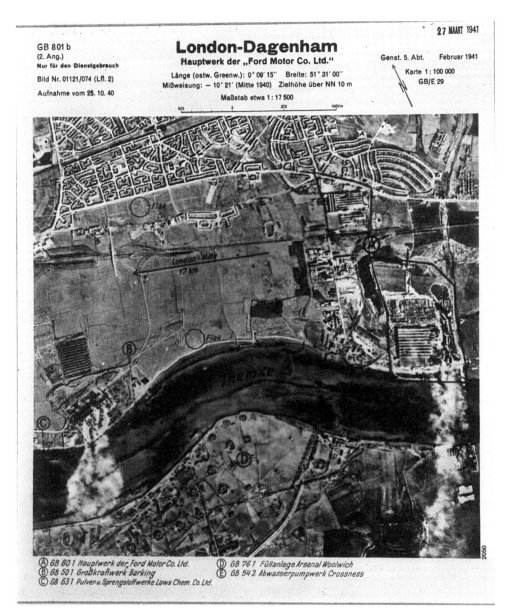

GB 801 b
(2. Ang.)
Nur für den Dienstgebrauch

Bild Nr. 01121/074 (Lfl. 2)

Aufnahme vom 25. 10. 40

27 MAART 1941

London-Dagenham
Hauptwerk der „Ford Motor Co. Ltd."

Länge (ostw. Greenw.): 0° 09' 15"   Breite: 51° 31' 00"
Mißweisung: — 10° 21' (Mitte 1940)   Zielhöhe über NN 10 m

Maßstab etwa 1 : 17 500

Genst. 5. Abt.   Februar 1941

Karte 1 : 100 000
GB/E 29

Ⓐ GB 801 Hauptwerk der Ford Motor Co. Ltd.
Ⓑ GB 501 Großkraftwerk Barking
Ⓒ GB 631 Pulver-u. Sprengstoffwerke Laws Chem. Co. Ltd.
Ⓓ GB 761 Füllanlage Arsenal Woolwich
Ⓔ GB 542 Abwasserpumpwerk Crossness

Found in a crashed German bomber, this aerial photograph taken in October 1940, a few days after a high explosive bomb had burst in the radiator and press shops, clearly shows the Dagenham factory, which was hit by some 200 bombs during the war.

accelerating production of Ford tractors proved essential to cope with the demand. Although Henry Ford had made a gentleman's agreement with the flamboyant Irish inventor Harry Ferguson to build Ferguson system tractors incorporating a three-point linkage and hydraulic lift mechanism, Dagenham steadfastly withstood orders from Dearborn to replace the existing Fordson with the new Ferguson design. When Ferguson demanded to be made a director of Ford-Britain so that he could force his tractor into production, he was rebuffed by the entire British board. 'It has been explained to him why it is impossible during the war, and neither he nor Henry Ford nor Jesus Christ can alter it,' Dearborn was robustly informed. And when Dagenham eventually phased out the Fordson, in early 1945, it was replaced by the British-designed Fordson Major and not the Ferguson, which

Dagenham in war paint: the main office and production buildings are camouflaged and the huge neon logo has been taken down from the power house 'for the duration'. However, lamented the company, 'the Thames could not be camouflaged'.

Women workers were first employed at Dagenham in March 1941. Most, acording to company records, had previously worked in tailoring and tobacco factories, in domestic service or behind shop counters, or were 'from the receptionist class'.

was later taken up by Standard after Henry Ford and Ferguson had expensively parted.

The first wartime contract was hardly spectacular, yet it was of great importance. Dagenham-built V8 engines were used to generate electricity to power the 'de-gaussing' rings fitted to a number of Wellington bombers, to neutralise the magnetic mines laid by the Germans across Britain's harbour entrances from the end of October; similar 'de-gaussing' apparatus was also fitted to merchant ships.

Dagenham called in camouflage experts from the Royal Air Force to help disguise the factory, even though there was no way of hiding the River Thames. They painted the roofs of the factory to look like marshland with tracks running through it, blacked out the skylights, the blast furnace and the slag heap, and extinguished the jetty lighting.

The king and queen took a close interest in the work of the Ford Emergency Food Vans, one of which was allocated to feed the workers on the king's farm at Sandringham. Here Queen Elizabeth inspects a mobile canteen and 5cwt refreshment van operated by the NAAFI.

'V for Victory' – and for 'voluntary', for the Emergency Food Vans were staffed by the Women's Voluntary Services and maintained free of charge by the local Ford dealers.

The camouflage was hardly effective: a German bomber shot down in 1941 was found to be carrying an aerial photo of the works taken in October 1940 in which the 'Hauptwerk der Ford Motor Co. Ltd' was clearly marked and the telltale plume of smoke from the power station chimneys was clear to see.

For Ford, as for many other businesses, the 'Phoney War' suddenly became reality after Winston Churchill succeeded Neville Chamberlain as Prime Minister in May 1940. Sizeable orders for military vehicles were received, and plans were laid for using the production capacity of Dagenham to the full – 'and if possible beyond'.

Even the by-products of Dagenham had a vital role to play: huge quantities of toluene and xylole were used to make explosives, zylene was used to manufacture aircraft varnish, and in a single year over 2 million gallons of tar, 5.2 million pounds of sulphate of ammonia and 380,000 gallons of motor benzole were produced for the war effort. By the end of the war, tarmac derived from the Dagenham furnace slag had surfaced the runways and dispersal areas of no fewer than 56 airfields scattered over 10 counties.

The additional demands that were placed on

St Paul's Cathedral stands defiant among the ruins of the Blitz – and the Ford food vans of the Salvation Army are on hand to sustain the salvage workers.

Dagenham called for more machine tools, and these were in short supply, as were forgings and other parts made outside Ford's factory. While some existing machines could be adapted and modified, there were still some needs that could not be met, and to solve this problem, Dagenham called on the parent company in Dearborn. While America was still neutral, there was a willingness to supply any country that could pay for its products and take them away. Dearborn was ready, willing and able to supply whatever Dagenham needed, and to save time and beat Germany's U-boat blockade, urgent supplies of Dearborn-made machine tools were flown across the Atlantic by bomber. One advanced touch was the use of 'radio photographs' – a primitive form of fax transmission – to transmit dimensioned drawings of urgently-needed components to Dearborn.

There was a bizarre twist to Ford's 'positive neutrality': in 1940 Thornhill Cooper – an exotic figure who in the 1930s had run Dagenham's Egyptian subsidiary and earned the nickname 'the uncrowned King of Alexandria' – represented Ford-Britain at a European management conference in neutral Sweden. When the German delegate, Erhard Vitger from Cologne, suggested a souvenir photograph with his colleagues from England, Denmark and Sweden, they jokingly raised their arms in a 'Heil Hitler' salute. After the war, the American occupation forces investigating

'The Ford vans were worth their weight in gold to us,' said a grateful ARP official. 'I don't know where we should have been without them.' This bombed-out family echoed his sentiments.

Cologne's role in the war saw the picture and failed to see the joke; Vitger – though technically neutral as a Danish citizen who had never taken German nationality – had some difficult questions to answer.

Before Pearl Harbor brought the US into the war in December 1941, the British and German companies were free to communicate via the mother company in

This Ford Emergency Food Van was a gift from the ladies of Boston, Massachusetts to the ladies of Cheltenham: Queen Mary, not used to taking tea in a mug from a mobile canteen, doesn't quite know what to make of it all.

Even in the depths of the war there was time for Christmas – and Ford put on a Christmas show in 1943 for the families of its Dagenham workers.

The Admiralty originally considered using Lagonda V12 engines for its motor torpedo boats, but when it discovered that the complex power units took 18 hours to strip down, opted for the easily serviceable Ford V8 instead.

Dagenham's comprehensive in-plant medical services had a full-time staff of 30, including state registered nurses and St John's Ambulance men. During the war it ran a full out-patient service, whose list grew to exceed that of St Bartholomew's Hospital – and Bart's had the largest outpatients' list in London.

Dearborn. Both dutifully filed their monthly production reports as though there was no war, although examination of those reports in the company's Dearborn archives suggests that no information of any use to the opposing side was transmitted.

There was, incidentally, at least one other wartime Ford conference on neutral Swedish soil: in 1944 Dagenham's advertising manager Clayton Young flew to Sweden in the dark, unpressurised belly of a Mosquito high-speed bomber. It was a traumatic experience and after the return flight he sickened and died.

A little known episode of Dagenham's wartime history occurred in 1940, when Ford evacuated 150 of its employees' children to Canada. Recalls David Leon, who as a four-year-old was billeted with the family of Wallace Campbell, the head of Ford-Canada in Windsor, Ontario: 'My father was Ford's assistant export manager. We travelled aboard three ships – I and my six-year-old brother were on the *Duchess*

of Atholl. There were 15 children staying with the Campbells and we had an incredible time. We could not have been treated better, though we were away from our parents for four-and-a-half years, which was a very long time at that age. I was taken ill while I was there, and my parents were kept advised of my progress via telegrams sent to Lord Perry, who was personally involved in the scheme.'

The demands of war forced Dagenham to change its rigid policy of only employing men in the factory, 'being consciously desirous of promoting the establishment of a home and the creation of a family'. But as more and more men were called up, the company was forced to employ women on the production line, starting in March 1941, and by September that year, there were 1,100 female workers at Dagenham. By the end of the war, some 10 per cent of the 34,000 workers at Dagenham were female, although it has to be said that once peace was declared and the male workers came back, there was no further place for women on

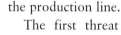

the production line.

The first threat to Dagenham from the Luftwaffe came at the height of the Battle of Britain, during the afternoon of 7 September 1940. The Ford football team was playing a home match against Leyton on the company's sports ground north of the factory when air raid sirens drowned the sound of the referee's whistle. The spirit of the phoney war lingered:

no-one took any notice until they heard gunfire and the irregular drone of German bomber engines, followed by a rain of shrapnel and, as the last of the players and spectators reached the air raid shelters, a 'veritable fleet of bombers flying majestically above the Thames' came into view.

There were some 120 bombers in the raid, flying in three separate waves with an equal number of fighters accompanying them, just one section of the massive aerial armada of almost a thousand fighters and bombers unleashed against England that

Overpaid, overfed and over here? A Ford V8 canteen serving American troops dispenses doughnuts to doughboys.

Even before America entered the war, Ford-US was supplying vehicles to meet the increased demands of war, like these American V8 ambulances which went into service in 1940.

The act that brought the house down: a Dagenham-built Fordson tractor demolishes an unsafe building after a German air raid on London on 29 December 1940.

day by Reichsmarschall Herman Goering.

But their target that day was not Ford, but the oil refineries at nearby Purfleet, which erupted in flame and smoke as the players resumed their match. Seven times they had to dive for the shelters, but the referee kept careful note of the time lost during air raids, and Ford and Leyton played their match to a finish: Ford won 4–2.

So that production could continue as smoothly as possible during the period of the air raids, Ford introduced a system known as 'the alarm within the alert' in which the spotters stationed on the roof of the factory to give warning of approaching enemy aircraft were linked by telephone to the anti-aircraft batteries at Barking to the west and Whalebone Lane to the north-east.

Aircraft movements were plotted by the factory's Air Raid Precautions staff in a room next to the chief spotter's post, and only if the planes seemed to be heading

One of many thousands of trucks sent over in kit form and assembled at Dagenham-controlled depots across England, this V8 was equipped in the field with an improvised mounting for an anti-aircraft machine gun saw service in North Africa.

These are some of nearly 14,000 Bren gun carriers built by Ford at Dagenham during World War Two. Almost 44,000 more were built by Ford-Canada. Other companies built these 'universal carriers' as well, but every one was powered by a Ford V8 engine.

For the first time Ford-Britain had to accept union membership during the war: in the early days of trade union representation at Ford, workers joined this protest in support of a colleague jailed for demonstrating against the release from jail of fascist leader Sir Oswald Mosley.

Land girls incongruously seek directions in the East End of London: even though Dagenham had forcefully refused Dearborn's orders to build tractors to the designs of Harry Ferguson, Lord Perry accepted 5,000 American-built Ford-Ferguson tractors like this example to plough up grassland and help the 'nation's food campaign'.

toward the Ford factory were its sirens sounded. The consequent reduction in production 'down time' was eventually estimated to amount to several thousand hours.

The spotters, incidentally, were mostly commissionaires, stationed in pairs at nine strategic points around the factory site, with members of Ford's fire brigade, which had two fully-equipped fire engines and a trailer pump, always on duty nearby.

The first direct hit on the factory came on 8 September 1940, when three railway wagons standing near the plant's weighbridge were destroyed. Ten days later the factory had its first fatality as a result of enemy action when an oil bomb killed an employee named Reeves; three days after that a string of incendiary bombs fell right across the south-west corner of the Dagenham site. 'It looked for certain that the whole place would be burnt up,' said an eyewitness. The Ford fire brigade, however, was more than equal to the emergency, and managed to extinguish 147 burning bombs with hoses and sandbags – and a steel helmet, dropped over an incendiary by a resourceful fireman.

Surreality was never allowed to get in the way of a good publicity photograph. Of course the Ford mobile canteens did sterling work during air raids, but how would these air raid wardens drink their tea through their gas masks?

Queues were a part of everyday life in wartime, but the sight of a photographer recording the Ministry of Labour's smart Model B Ford loudspeaker van proves a greater distraction.

Bombed out: but the Ford emergency food vans were on hand to provide a reviving meal. They played a vital role during the V1 flying bomb raids, when *Darling Buds of May* author H.E. Bates wrote of 'the kindnesses and the untold millions of cups of tea that helped to make life tolerable in its time'.

The Briggs factory was also hit by fire bombs that night, but a major catastrophe was averted when a quick-thinking fireman swept a cluster of incendiaries off the highly-inflam-mable oil and paint stores with a high-pressure hose so that they exploded harmlessly against an outside wall.

Dagenham's worst night of the Blitz was 16 October 1940, when a para-chute mine fell through the roof of the radiator production building, killing a number of employees and bursting the gas and water mains. The resulting flood was so severe that the wood block floor began to float, moving up and down like waves on the sea beneath the feet of the fire fighters. Nevertheless, the delay to production was only a couple of days, with an improvised cover across the hole in the roof within a matter of hours.

No controversy over empty plinths then: a Ford B articulated truck takes Trafalgar Square's statues to safe storage during the Blitz.

By then, Ford had been working at full war pressure for several months, and by the end of June 1941 it was turning out 130 vehicles a day. The majority of these

were the WOT2 15cwt troop carrier, powered by the V8 engine, along with the 7V forward-control 2.5 ton V8 truck and the E83W 10cwt van, powered by the ubiquitous 1172cc Ford Ten engine. By VE Day, Ford had built 184,579 trucks and vans.

June 1941 also marked the production of Ford's first four-wheel drive truck, developed by Dagenham's tiny engineering staff. In pre-war days, all engineering had been carried out in Dearborn, and it was only just before the outbreak of war that Dagenham had taken on a few commercial vehicle engineers to work on its specialised truck range. In 1939, the entire engineering staff numbered just 100. Demand for four-wheel-drive trucks had become a priority once the Eighth Army began fighting Rommel's Afrika Korps in North Africa, and the Dagenham engineers had the difficult task of designing a four-wheel-drive model – Ford's first 'in-house' 4x4 on either side of the Atlantic – that had to go into production straight off the drawing board, for the demands of war meant that there was no time for experiment or testing.

Remarkably, the only changes necessary to the design were 'most minor' and they could easily be incorporated into the vehicles without slowing production. A sincere tribute came from an airman who drove Ford vehicles in Egypt and Tripoli: 'Many

It seems there were still those who believed that the motor vehicle was just a passing phase in warfare, but even they used a Ford V8 horsebox – this one is in South Africa, probably assembled there from parts shipped from Dagenham – to move their equine charges around.

'Making tracks for Victory' runs the original caption to this stirring photograph of Ford-built Bren gun carriers 'roaring into action over the dunes of the Western Desert'.

From the grins and the graffiti, it looks as though the war is coming to an end. The Fordson 7V Thames truck is one of many pressed into war service in addition to the more than 180,000 military trucks built at Dagenham during the hostilities.

Unveiled in 1942 by Minister of Information Brendan Bracken, this mural above the entrance to the Ford showroom at 88 Regent Street depicting 'Service uniforms, past and present' was the work of the artist Helen McKie, 'the Famous Portrayer of Naval and Military Types'.

times I have heard the expression "If it wasn't for Henry Ford, I don't know how we should have got along." A great part of the North African victory was due to the boys and girls from Dagenham.'

Another unsolicited testimonial came from an unexpected quarter, when orders from Feldmarschall Erwin Rommel were intercepted at the beginning of 1942: 'For desert reconnaissance only captured trucks are to be used, since German trucks stick in the sand too often.' This is not too surprising, for in the 1980s the former public relations manager of Ford-Belgium, who worked with the Resistance after his country was occupied, told me that the trucks built under German supervision for the Afrika Korps in Ford's Antwerp factory were sabotaged in many subtle ways: 'The truck

bodies were primitive time-bombs, for they were made from unseasoned, damp wood, and when the trucks went into Africa and were put in the sun, the bodywork burst open and broke; these were things which could only be checked after so many months or weeks.

'The drivers who used to deliver the trucks to the German depots used to substitute steering columns made of very thin metal, which would break if any strain was put on them. The

genuine steering columns were taken home by the employees, painted green, and used as garden stakes!'

Another Dagenham product that was used with great success in the desert war was the V8 Utility Car, a metal-bodied estate car running on especially large tyres. From 1942–45 one well-travelled example, which served in

North Africa, Malta, Sicily, Italy and Austria, was used by Air Chief Marshal (later Lord) Tedder, Air Marshal Sir Arthur Coningham and Air Vice-Marshals Broadhurst, Dixon and Foster. In August 1945, Air Vice-Marshal Foster declared: 'Though somewhat battered externally, it is still mechanically absolutely sound and in regular use.'

Ford Utility Cars were also used by the staff officers of the Eighth Army, and one took its commanding officer General Montgomery all the way from El Alamein to Tunis. Later, Dagenham also built Monty's

'Digging for Victory' with the aid of an imported Ford-Ferguson tractor (the design was later built in Britain by Standard): the aircraft in the background is a Rolls-Royce Kestrel-engined Miles Master I trainer.

famous caravan, which he used as his mobile headquarters during 'Operation Overlord' when the Allies landed in Normandy after the D-Day operation of 1944.

'Since I came over here I have been using it to the full as my operations room,' he wrote to Ford. 'There is no doubt that you have produced a most excellent vehicle.'

Amazingly, Ford engines and spares also kept other makes of vehicle running during the African campaign. 'I have seen armoured cars of the 1922 vintage built by Rolls-Royce, which have stood up to much rough usage in the Middle East, but have at last come to grief, completely fitted out with Ford engines and spare parts, and then going into action again as good as new,' wrote a Tank Regiment officer. 'Given

The National Fire Service used Ford V8 fire tenders and trailer pumps like this to deal with the after-effects of the Blitz. The NFS also had a fleet of Ford Thames truck-based mobile kitchens.

Narrow squeak in the Western Desert – a Ford V8 truck of the British infantry advances through a German minefield in Libya under heavy shellfire.

good workmanship in the materials he has available, the British soldier in the desert can, with a little ingenuity, put on their wheels again most of the vehicles that come in for repair.'

One of the cornerstones of the Ford manufacturing operation had always been the company's skill in metallurgy, and in March 1940 the company's laboratory formulated a special steel for tank tracks, which were being produced by the Dagenham foundry at the rate of 130 tons a week by 1942. By the end of the war Ford had produced some 6 million track links. However, an extra demand from the government for tracks for Bren gun carriers proved to be beyond even the Dagenham foundry's capacity.

The Carden-Loyd 'universal carrier' had been invented in the 1920s by two cyclecar designers, John Valentine Carden and Vivian Loyd, who had joined forces to develop tracked military vehicles. Their light carrier, which steered by deflecting its tracks, proved so successful that the Carden-Loyd company was bought out by the giant Vickers-Armstrong group in 1928. It was eventually developed into the famous Bren gun carrier, for which Ford supplied V8 engines, axles and frames, but during wartime five other companies were also producing the carriers. To meet the extra demand, Ford searched for extra foundry capacity, and in October 1940 took over the old Flavel kitchen range factory at Leamington Spa, which dated back to 1777. A new highly-mechanised foundry was built along similar lines to that at Dagenham, and six months after Ford had taken over the site, it produced its first tracks, using a special steel originally developed at Dagenham to make crankshafts, rather than the malleable iron used up till then.

Since the carriers used many Ford components, it was a logical step for Ford to make the complete vehicles, and in September 1941 the company was awarded a contract to produce 4,500 carriers. The Ministry of Supply asked for these to be supplied at the rate of 25 a week and Ford was horrified.

'With our capacity, we can make at least a hundred a week, and we do not believe in running our factory except at the highest possible pitch,' the company scolded the men from the ministry, who eventually yielded to common sense. The first carrier came off the specially installed production lines at Dagenham in February 1942 and in April 1944 the 10,000th left the factory. By the end of the war, Dagenham had built nearly 14,000 Bren gun carriers, and every light carrier in every theatre of war had either been built by or was powered by Ford.

Dagenham established many 'outposts' to increase its war output. The company's Lincoln depot on the Great West Road, once the British base of that most aristocratic of French cars, the Delage, was transformed into a rebuilding and repair depot, which by October 1944 had carried out 26,200 overhauls. Vehicles shipped over from Canada and the US were assembled in a tram shed in Wigan, where the first jeep to arrive in Britain was assembled in June 1942.

Later on, the airship shed at Cardington, which had once housed the ill-fated R101, was taken over, along with a warehouse in Barking, to provide extra assembly capacity. Ford dealers also provided assembly and repair facilities.

Moreover, Dagenham supplied spare parts and trained army drivers in field maintenance techniques. It also carried out valuable work in waterproofing using a material called Trinadite. Under a test against other waterproofed trucks, Ford vehicles had to run for 200 miles and then run a mile in the sea with the engine submerged before continuing on land. The only group of vehicles to come through the test intact was the six-strong Ford truck team, driven by men in bathing suits.

This Ford-developed waterproofing system, which proved invaluable in Allied landing operations, had its finest hour when it was used on the vehicles that took part in the D-Day landings in June 1944.

On the home front, Ford gave tremendous help to those affected by the air raids. At the beginning of the war, V8 mobile canteens equipped with tea urns and pie ovens were built for the Salvation Army, the YMCA, the Church Army and the Society of Friends. Some of these served with the original expeditionary force and at least one, evacuated with the army from Dunkirk, returned to France four years later with the D-Day landings.

However, when the raids became severe, far more mobile canteens were needed to provide food for people made homeless or deprived of the means of cooking, rescue workers and demolition staff and outdoor workers of all kinds.

Lord Perry told Henry Ford about the seriousness of the situation, and Ford and his son Edsel offered to fund a fleet of 350 fully-equipped Emergency Food Vans (EFVs) based on the Ford 10cwt van chassis. Ultimately, further donations brought

The 100,000th wartime Ford truck – a four-wheel-driven V8 – nears completion on the Dagenham assembly line. By the end of the war almost 90,000 more trucks had been built, along with 262,007 V8 engines.

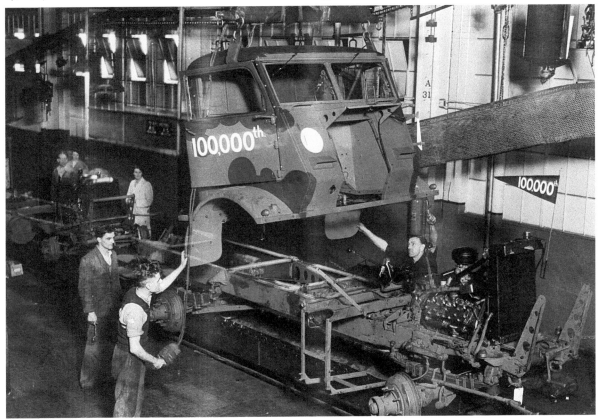

Ford V8 engines powered the winches for the barrage balloon defence of Britain's cities which played such a vital role during the V1 'doodlebug' flying bomb attacks in 1944.

the EFV fleet up to 450 canteens, which were stationed throughout England and maintained free of charge by Ford dealers.

King George VI had an EFV to take hot midday meals to the farm workers on his Sandringham Estate, while former Prime Minister David Lloyd George used another to have meals delivered to the 'hungry sons and daughters of the soil' working on his farm at Churt on the Surrey-Hampshire border.

When the Germans carried out their infamous 'Baedeker' raids on Britain's historic cities in the summer of 1942, the EFVs performed sterling service. After the raid on Norwich, an ARP official told Ford: 'The Ford vans have been worth their weight in gold. I don't know where we should have been without them.'

A valuable side-effect of Dagenham's production efficiency was that the factory's engine plant produced more engines than were actually needed for production. This had led to the setting up of the Ford Industrial Engines division, which supplied engines to a wide range of customers, from builders of stationary plant to specialist sports car manufacturers and boat builders.

This profitable sideline came into its own in wartime, when over 250,000 Ford

V8 engines were used in military vehicles and other installations, such as boats. The Admiralty equipped its motor torpedo boats with V8 engines, and two V8 engines powered thousands of the assault craft used to take troops ashore in the Allied landings in Sicily, Italy and Normandy.

'Operation Archery' on 27 December 1941 was an early and significant use of these landing craft, when combined British forces raided the German naval base at Vaagso and Lofotens on the west Nor-wegian coast to destroy enemy shipping and shore batteries. With air cover from Bristol Blenheim light bombers of No.404 Squadron of the Royal Canadian Air Force, and protected by a 6-inch cruiser and destroyers, two British commando units of a special Service Brigade, backed up by a detachment of Canadian infantry, went ashore in Ford-powered landing craft which had been unloaded from two infantry landing ships. They completely surprised the German defenders, engaging in wild fighting in warehouses and fish factories. It was British bravado at its best: Major Jack Churchill played *The March of the Cameron Men* on his bagpipes in full view of the enemy as the battle raged.

Dagenham's foundry workers raised £7,500 to buy this Spitfire *Go to It* for the Royal Air Force. Its pilot, 30-year-old Squadron Leader Donald Carlson DFC, was the commanding officer of 154 (Motor Industries) Squadron, based at Hornchurch, Ford's local RAF station.

The raid was a huge success: the British sank five German merchant ships, destroyed the German-run factories, took 98 prisoners and cracked the German base's safe – which contained just $10.

The effect of Operation Archery on the course of the war was dramatic: infuriated by the raid, Hitler set about turning the Atlantic coast into 'Fortress Europe', ordering forts to be built from Norway to the Pyrenees. He ordered the German Navy to send its mightiest ships to Norway, thus removing them from the Atlantic sea lanes. Norway's defences were augmented by an extra 18,000 German troops – who never saw action. The Nazis even formed a panzer division in Norway, despite its well-known lack of roads.

Tractors from Dagenham played a key role in the 'Dig for Victory' campaign, when millions of acres were ploughed up to free Britain from its dependence on imported food. Following the May 1939 suggestion by Ford to the Ministry of Agriculture that a 'tractor pool' should be created, its company secretary Stanford Cooper told the Ministry that it should pay a bonus of £1 10s (£1.50) compensation an acre to farmers who ploughed up grassland to sow arable crops. The Ministry agreed – but raised the bonus to £2.

This encouraged farmers to plough up their land – and encouraged them to buy a Fordson tractor to do it with. And of course the sharp mind of Stanford Cooper had

Employed by Perry for his language skills, Maurice Buckmaster managed the Paris office of Ford-France during the 1930s. When war came, Colonel Buckmaster ran the French section of the Special Operations Executive, which organised resistance against the occupying German forces. Typically, he was able to contact his friend Robert Peugeot through the French underground to ensure that no night shift was on duty when the Allies bombed the Peugeot factory in Western France, keeping French casualties to a minimum. Post-war, he headed Dagenham's public relations office, but played himself in the 1950 film *Odette*, the story of one of his most heroic French agents, portrayed by Anna Neagle. Trevor Howard and Peter Ustinov also starred, and are seen here with Maurice Buckmaster in this on-set group portrait.

created a flexible short-term credit plan that made that purchase easy. The scheme was a brilliant success, for it meant that there was no need for the Government to subsidise the purchase of a single tractor. Moreover, the company took back tractors requiring overhaul, had them reconditioned by the dealers and sold them to poorer farmers at affordable prices. Between September 1939 and the end of the war in Europe, no fewer than 137,483 Fordsons had been produced at Dagenham, and 85 per cent of the tractors in use in Britain were Fordsons. At the peak of production, a tractor left the line every 18 minutes. Ford had even managed to develop a new and more efficient tractor known as the Fordson Major, which went into production in March 1945.

The tractors in service were kept running by a special priority spares scheme, whereby urgent spares ordered by telegram were sent anywhere in the country by the next train from Dagenham.

In addition to building tractors, Ford also played its own part in digging for victory, putting 170 acres of land at Dagenham, known as the Lake Farm, under cultivation and selling much of its produce to its employees. At the same time, Ford's Institute of Agricultural Engineering at Boreham, which had been training young men to become 'mechanical farmers' for several years, was used to train thousands of members of the Women's Land Army. The picture of pretty land girls driving Fordsons across rolling fields became a potent image of 'the earth which saved England'. The factory also organised its own Home Guard, which by December 1941 had grown to a strength of 400 men, armed against possible invasion by German troops with the standard-issue 8ft long pikes.

Quite apart from the £2.6 million in War Savings Certificates subscribed to by the employees at Dagenham, a subscription started in the foundry raised £7,500 to buy a Spitfire for the Royal Air Force. Named *Go to It*, the Spitfire was donated to 154 (Motor Industries) Squadron, based at Ford's local RAF station, Hornchurch, where it was flown by the commanding officer, Squadron Leader Donald Carlson, a New Zealander who was awarded the Distinguished Flying Cross in September 1942.

Carlson and *Go to It* scored their first victory on 30 July 1942, when 154 Squadron escorted Hurricanes on a disastrous bombing mission to St Omer, which was jumped by large numbers of enemy fighters as it crossed the French coast. Eight Spitfires and three Hurricanes were lost for five Focke-Wulf 190s destroyed, one being downed by Carlson over St Omer.

It was another Spitfire from RAF Hornchurch that saved Dagenham from imminent destruction on 18 June 1944. It was less than a week since Hitler had begun his last-ditch 'doodle-bug' attacks on England with the V1 flying bomb, and the ARP spotters on top of the factory were alarmed to see a V1 heading straight toward the factory with two Spitfires on its tail. As the spotters heard that unforgettable irregular throb of the doodle-bug's pulse-jet engine getting nearer, the Spitfires opened fire on the V1, which gradually began to heel over and change course. Dodging the overhead power cables that spanned the Thames near the factory, one of the Spitfires administered the *coup de grace* with a quick burst of cannon fire, forcing the flying bomb to plunge vertically into the river, where it exploded harmlessly.

'The doodle-bug was travelling straight toward the jetty,' recorded the chief spotter, 'and if it had not been turned it would have hit the factory.' It had been a truly narrow escape. There would be five more 'near misses' by doodle-bugs and seven by the even more deadly V2 rockets – the last falling so close that the explosion broke most of the windows in the plant's main office building – before Dagenham's war ended.

Chapter Five

DAGENHAM FLIES NORTH

ERHAPS Dagenham's most remarkable contribution to World War Two was its creation of a brand-new 'shadow factory' at Urmston, not far from the old Trafford Park plant in Manchester, for the mass-production of Rolls-Royce Merlin supercharged V12 aeroengines.

Though Ford had not been part of the shadow factory scheme of the late 1930s, the company was quickly called in by the authorities when the need for more aeroengines became apparent during the 'phoney war'.

In peacetime, Rowland Smith had hosted the then commandant of the RAF Staff College, Air Vice-Marshal Sir Wilfred Freeman, and his officers at Dagenham. The visit made a tremendous impression on Freeman, who when war broke out was made assistant chief of the Air Staff.

Freeman recognised that when Hitler did move against England, the Royal Air Force would find itself stretched to the limit. Its prime need would be engines to

Rowland Smith *(seated, centre)* plans Ford's aeroengine factory with his management team. H.A. Denne *(seated, left)* was deputy controller. Works manager Alf Haselden *(standing, right)* joined Trafford Park in 1912 after working for Ford in Detroit. He later supervised Ford's plants in Bordeaux and Paris, becoming Dagenham works manager in 1934.

combat the Luftwaffe. Realising the very high degree of accuracy to which the Ford factory worked, he acted on a hunch and called a meeting with Smith and Lord Perry. The three met in Whitehall on 31 October 1939 and Freeman made a suggestion, which sounded almost heretical. 'We want to know if you will make [Rolls-Royce] Merlin engines for the Air Ministry,' he asked Smith.

'Yes,' was Smith's confident answer. 'How many do you want?'

'Four hundred a month!' replied Freeman.

At that time, only the Rolls-Royce factories at Derby and Crewe were producing the Merlin, and two days later Smith and a group of Ford managers were in Derby to meet Rolls-Royce's managing director E.W. (later Lord) Hives to work out the details of the project.

Since the Ford works at Dagenham was already fully engaged on war work, Smith needed to build and equip a shadow factory to mass-produce the complex supercharged 27-litre V12 Merlin.

Called to a meeting in Harrogate a fortnight later, Smith told Air Ministry officials that he reckoned the cost of the new factory would be £7 million: it turned out to be a singularly accurate estimate.

Eight possible sites were inspected, but it was probably more than a coincidence that the final choice fell on the Manchester suburb of Urmston, not far from the site of Ford's first British factory, for Lord Perry still retained a fond affection for Trafford Park.

Arrangements were made for selected Ford workers to move to Derby to plan the manufacturing and supply details, Rolls-Royce providing suitable office accommodation. Here a team of 190 engineers and mechanics studied how the Merlin was made and established a purchase department to buy raw material and sub-contract component work.

As part of their training, each man had to work on the fitting benches to become proficient in making every component of the engine; by the time they had finished, each man had built a complete Merlin engine and was judged ready to instruct inexperienced workers at the new factory in the complex task of building aeroengines.

A basic problem quickly arose.

Clutching a roll of blueprints, Ford's chief engineer protested to his opposite number at Rolls-Royce: 'We can't make the Merlin to these drawings!'

'What's the matter?' came the response. 'I suppose you can't achieve the accuracy.'

'On the contrary, the tolerances are far too wide for us,' replied the Ford man. 'We make motor cars far more accurately than this. Every part on our car engines has to be interchangeable with the same

This was the aeroengine plant's north-west canteen. No-one seems to be pocketing the spoons, though in February 1945 the company announced that 'owing to the heavy losses reported by the caterers, employees would be required to being their own cutlery for use in the canteens'.

part on any other engine, and hence all parts have to be made with extreme accuracy, far closer than you use. That is the only way we can achieve mass production.'

So Ford redrew all the working blueprints to meet its standards. Much the same thing happened on the other side of the Atlantic, where Packard in Detroit also had to redraw the blueprints to its standards, though oddly the two motor giants didn't get together and agree to use the same drawings or tolerances.

Perversely, Britain had asked Henry Ford before turning to Packard, but the cranky old man snapped that it was not the policy of the United States (which was then neutral) to become involved in the war in Europe, adding: 'Britain has enough automotive manufacturers to construct the damn engines themselves.'

He later tried to cover himself by averring: 'I turned down the business not because it was British but because the engine was antiquated…'

Old Henry's attitude seems to suggest that Dagenham was acting independently and had not sought clearance from Dearborn, though by that time Mr Ford was 77 years old and increasingly unpredictable. Part of his reason for refusing to build Merlins in America was his hatred of Democrat President Franklin D. Roosevelt: however, once the US entered the war, Ford built a huge plant at Willow Run, Michigan, capable of producing four-engined Liberator bombers at the rate of one an hour.

Anyway, whether Dearborn knew or not, Ford-Britain already had more than enough problems of its own when it came to producing the Merlin, which had been designed for hand assembly rather than line assembly. Not only did Rolls-Royce use four different screw thread forms on the Merlin, but they had also applied their own modifications to the thread forms, meaning that there were almost 140 different kinds of thread used throughout the engine!

Another problem with the Rolls-Royce way of doing things was that the drawings did not record running changes, tolerances or levels of tightness required, for at Derby all these were left to oral instructions to skilled fitters, who then used their considered judgement when assembling the engine.

That was no use to Ford, which would have to train its operatives, and the Air Ministry gave the company permission to use part of the old Ford factory in First

Left: Assembling Merlin cylinder blocks to the crankcase at the Urmston plant. The first Ford-built Merlin left the production line dead on schedule in June 1942, to the 'warmest admiration' of Lt-Col J.T.C. Moore-Brabazon, the Minister of Aircraft Production (and holder of pilot's licence Number One, issued in 1910).

Right: Installing the complex crankshaft and conrod assembly: the Merlin had Rolls-Royce's typical marine-type fork-and-blade connecting rods running on plain bearings. There was enough bronze in the bearings of each Merlin to mint 1,720 old penny pieces, and never was £7 3s 4d better spent!

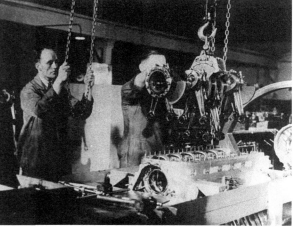

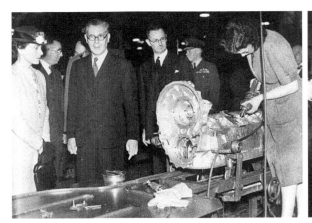

Avenue, Trafford Park, as a drawing office and tool room. Here work began on mass-producing the Merlin, with Ford staff turning out the necessary drawings and gauges and planning the engineering methods needed. However, whereas Packard put 200 men on to the task of redesigning the Merlin for mass production, Ford initially had just 37, of whom nine were engineers and four were draughtsmen.

It was at around this time that the newly-appointed Minister of Aircraft Production, Lord Beaverbrook, appointed by Prime Minister Winston Churchill to provide the RAF with many more aircraft to replace losses and withstand the anticipated German invasion, was urgently seeking high-calibre industrial executives to help him in this vital task. One of the first names suggested to him was that of Patrick Hennessy, 'a most capable manager'.

Beaverbrook recalled: 'After this recommendation, I lost no time in asking Hennessy to come and see me. But his first response was discouraging. Hennessy said: "No, I cannot come in and help you. Already you have got Rowland Smith. Your ministry has involved us in a new plant in Manchester, making Rolls-Royce engines. In these conditions, it is quite impossible for me to leave my business."

'Naturally, I was not willing to accept defeat. I bombarded the position Hennessy had taken up, and I did so with a great deal of determination. And, in the situation prevailing at the time, I had powerful arguments to use.

'In the end, Hennessy consented to come in. As a matter of fact he found the pressure I could deploy quite irresistible. But to begin with I was doubtful about Hennessy. He had not come in willingly. He was a conscript. Would he be sulky?

'The answer came quickly – not at all! From the start he showed the ability I had been told I could expect from him. Very soon I called him in as a member of the Minister's Council.

'As for the value of his work at the Ministry, there is no necessity to speak of that. The record is there, plain for all to see, in the story of the Battle of Britain and how the losses suffered by the squadrons of the RAF during those fateful weeks were made up.

'For that victorious result, it is impossible to give too high praise to Sir Patrick Hennessy.' (Hennessy had been knighted in July 1941 in recognition of his work at the MAP.)

Left: Works controller Rowland Smith *(centre)* and manager W.J. Silverton show a VIP party round the aeroengine works. The sight of women on the production line was still a novelty, even in wartime.

Right: Initial assembly of the first engines to leave the Ford aeroengine works. Early engines suffered testbed failures through valve stems picking up blemishes in their storage skips and sticking when they got hot, but the problem was cured by placing the valves for each engine in special stands.

'Final assembly' reads the original caption to this photograph. 'These Merlin engines will soon go to the Test House, where they are to be tried out under conditions which will reproduce the strain and stress of flight.'

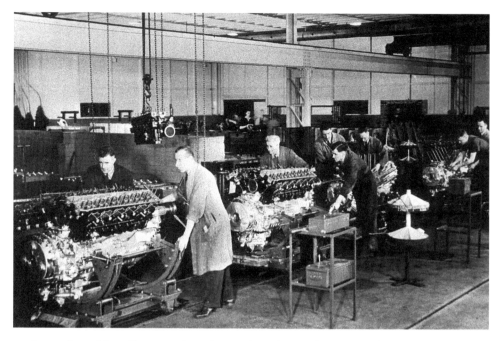

Apart from his valiant work to keep aircraft supplies going during the Battle of Britain, Hennessy's greatest contribution to the war effort during his time at the Ministry was his single-minded advocacy of an aircraft so radical in concept that its development programme was in constant danger of being cancelled by the authorities. This was the de Havilland DH 98 Mosquito, conceived as a high-speed bomber of all-wood construction without defensive armament, relying on its speed alone to evade intercepting fighters.

Mocked at first as 'Freeman's Folly' – Sir Wilfred Freeman was its only other high-level supporter – the Mosquito turned out to be one of the most outstanding and versatile aircraft of World War Two. So dependable, efficient and versatile was the 'Wooden Wonder' that the main criticism became that 'there were never enough Mosquitos available to go around' and it served with distinction as fast bomber, night fighter, fighter bomber and photo reconnaissance aircraft.

Coincidentally, the Mosquito was to be powered by the very engines that Ford would produce in the new Manchester factory, where construction work began in March 1940. Meanwhile, Ford installed a temporary tool-room in the old Trafford Park factory buildings, which shipped its first components to Derby in July.

In November, the new factory's first test bed was completed and production machinery began to be transferred from First Avenue to Urmston, where the first crankshafts and spare parts were produced several weeks before the roof was in place. By the end of the year, over 2,300 staff were working at the factory, most of them recruited locally.

In terms of labour relations, the Manchester aeroengine plant made Ford history. Since it was technically a government establishment under Ford management, it had to abide by undertakings made between the government and trade unions at the beginning of the war.

So in December 1941, when it signed an agreement with the Amalgamated Engineering Union, Ford-Britain had, for the first time in the company's history, to recognise trade unions. It was an easier transition than in America, where union recognition in 1941 had only been achieved after years of bitter conflict. Two years later Dagenham also recognised unions, although Perry stipulated that it was on condition that 'there shall be given ample scope for initiative and individual enterprise'.

Sadly, some of the union representatives failed to respond and in 1943 Dagenham experienced its first taste of 'industrial action', when a number of trade union activists occupied managerial offices.

The complex intake system on the 1,280hp Merlin XX incorporated two massive SU carburettors and a two-speed single-speed supercharger.

Ford's shadow factory was obviously a prime enemy target, and it was bombed for the first time on 22–23 December 1940, and again in March and May 1941. Though three people were killed in the May

Powered by the Merlin XX, the Mk II Hawker Hurricane is seen here in its 'Hurribomber' guise, with twin underwing bombs. The final Hurricane, serial PZ865, was not only powered by a Ford-built Merlin but also built in a factory at Langley, Bucks, which was taken over by Ford in 1949.

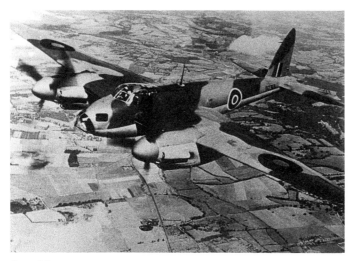

One of the most outstanding and versatile aircraft of World War Two, the de Havilland DH 98 Mosquito served with distinction as fast bomber, night fighter, fighter bomber and photo reconnaissance aircraft. This is one of many Mosquitos powered by Ford-built Merlins.

raid, work was scarcely interrupted and in June 1941 the first Ford-built Merlin came off the production lines. 'A splendid achievement,' wrote Lt-Col J.T.C. Moore-Brabazon, the Minister of Aircraft Production. Delivery to aircraft manufacturers began in August, when 13 Merlins were shipped. Some of the production tools had to be obtained from overseas. Three crankshaft machines were ordered from America, of which two were sunk by enemy action in the Atlantic.

When in 1943 Trafford Park needed precision jig borers accurate to .00005in, the only source of supply was found to be Switzerland, neutral but surrounded on all sides by Axis territory. Getting these machine tools to England, however, proved to be easier than anticipated. The Swiss, insisting on their right to trade even-handedly with all belligerents, simply delivered the jig borers via German-occupied France, and the Germans, who also needed Swiss tools, had to stand by and watch them travel into Spain (which was neutral, but sympathetic to the German cause) and thence by sea to England.

The workforce at Trafford Park grew steadily and at its peak numbered over 17,000, of whom 7,200 were women; fewer than 100 of them had any previous aeroengine experience and less than 300 had ever worked on car engines, yet not one of the more than 30,000 Merlins that was built at Trafford Park during the war failed the stringent acceptance tests of the Royal Air Force.

It was a remarkable demonstration of the accuracy and consistency of the Ford system of mass-production, for each engine was composed of 10,000 separate parts; moreover, many of the machines used in the Manchester factory had been designed by Ford. They worked to astoundingly precise limits: several thousand

Principal user of the Manchester-built Merlins was the Avro Lancaster heavy bomber, which achieved immortality through the famous 'Dam Buster' raid by 617 Squadron. Avro's factory at Chadderton, Manchester, was only a few miles from Ford's Urmston works.

of the measurements involved in Merlin manufacture were accurate to just one-fifth the thickness of a human hair. The 72 gear wheels used in each Merlin were made to these tolerances, which surpassed even the standards used in the watchmaking industry.

The five Merlins resulting from the first month's production cost

On 14 December 1945 Alf Haselden *(left)* was guest of honour at a dinner at Manchester's Piccadilly Hotel 'to commemorate achievements in Merlin production'. By the time the Ford plant closed on 23 March 1946, it had built over 30,000 Merlins, not one of which had failed the stringent RAF acceptance tests.

Visiting the Ford aeroengine factory are Stanford Cooper *(second from left)*, Ford-Britain's joint managing director, and J. Clayton Young *(right)*, its advertising manager, who died after a flight to an 'advertising conference' in Sweden in 1944 in the unpressurised belly of a Mosquito.

After the closure of the Manchester aeroengine plant in 1946, Ford employees who had been seconded there like Bill Lord *(left)* returned to Dagenham.

£5,640 each to build. When the target of 400 engines a month was passed in September 1942, the cost of a Merlin had fallen to £1,875. At its peak in the summer of 1944, the monthly output of the Ford factory was 900 engines a month and each Merlin cost just over £1,200 to build and the number of man-hours taken to build a Merlin had fallen from 10,000 to 2,727. 'We made them,' commented Rowland Smith, 'cheaper than anybody ever thought Merlins could be made.'

Ford built mostly the Mk XX variant of the Merlin, and over 12,500 of them were produced by 1944. Familiarly known as the 'Bomber Engine', many Mk XX Merlins were installed in the Lancaster bombers produced by that other great Manchester company, A.V. Roe & Co., and were also used in the Beaufighter, Defiant, Halifax and the Hurricane fighter.

Ford also built the Mk 22, which equipped the Lancaster and York; the Mk 24, used in Avro's Lancaster, Lancastrian and York; the Mk T24-2 for RAF Transport Command and the Mk 25, used exclusively in the de Havilland Mosquito twin-engined fighter.

Ford's contribution of over 30,000 engines out of around 150,000 Merlins made during the war by the five factories involved – three Rolls-Royce plants, Packard of Detroit and Ford – was a vital part of the Allied war effort.

When the 10,000th Ford-built Merlin left Manchester in November 1943, Rowland Smith – who was knighted the following year for his war work – received an unusually ebullient telegram from the Minister of Aircraft Production, the ascetic Stafford Cripps, who had visited the plant that January. 'Congratulations to management and workers on reaching the ten thousand mark: this is good going and I thank you all for the team work which has produced such splendid results. Merlins are doing a grand job in every theatre of war and fresh needs arise every day. We need all you can produce and more, so keep at it until victory is won.'

The Ford factory at Trafford Park did precisely that. Appropriately, Manchester Ford workers were chosen to head the first Battle of Britain parade through London on 26 September 1943. However, that wasn't the end of the story. Ford workers at Dagenham saved many thousands of pounds toward the war effort – during the 1943 Wings for Victory week alone their contributions totalled £45,558, enough to buy nine Spitfires.

Chapter Six

THE PERILS OF PEACETIME

CONSIDERING the total dedication of the company to war work, peacetime production at Dagenham was resumed remarkably quickly. By 25 May 1945 – just three weeks after VE Day – the factory was again geared up to produce cars to meet the anticipated post-war demand. The first complete post-war car, an 8hp Anglia, left the production line on 21 June and the company built its millionth vehicle, a 10hp Prefect, in 1946. Though both Morris and Austin had preceded Ford to the magic million, this was a sign that the Dagenham company was rapidly making up the ground lost during the 1920s when the £1 per horsepower tax had stopped Ford's advance dead in its tracks.

Ford-Britain had come through the war in a strong financial position, having set an average of £800,000 aside to cover depreciation and obsolescence every year since 1942. A further £600,000 had been allocated to a contingency fund and, even though profits were now subject to a crippling 50 per cent tax, Ford was recording an average profit of £633,000 a year.

Since Ford custom was that any expansion and re-equipping of the factory should be paid for out of retained earnings, Dagenham was in a good position to 'launch the peace offensive'.

There was, however, a singularly large fly in the ointment. The coalition government that had ruled during the war had collapsed on 23 May and Prime Minister Winston Churchill had dissolved parliament at the beginning of June. After a bitter and divisive election campaign, the Labour party had been elected by a landslide majority on a platform of 'social revolution' and nationalisation.

Almost as soon as the new parliament had sat for the first time in August, soon after the declaration of peace with Japan, Prime Minister Clement Attlee announced that the United States had abruptly terminated the Lend-Lease agreement signed in 1941, which let Britain use American military equipment without paying until after the war.

Now that the bills were coming in, Britons would have to start tightening their belts, and cuts in imports of food, cotton, tobacco and petrol would have to be made.

Motoring was not exactly a priority with the new administration. Indeed, the Labour Member of Parliament for Dagenham, many of whose constituents depended

Otto Brondum, managing
director of Ford-Sweden,
helps unload the first Ford
Anglia to arrive in Stockholm
after the war.

upon Ford for their living, bitterly condemned car ownership as an 'advantage of wealth'.

The Attlee government saw the motor industry as merely one way of redressing the yawning dollar gap, and not only kept the wartime purchase tax rate of 33.3 per cent in place, but also decreed that car makers must export 50 per cent of their output of cars and 33.3 per cent of commercials.

Naturally, there was a shortage of ships to move these export vehicles, and the government placed severe restrictions on materials supply and factory building.

To make life even more difficult, they wanted to retain the wartime 48-hour working week, while Perry was anxious to revert to the peacetime 40-hour five-day week.

When it was announced that the car industry would be permitted to sell only 120,000 new cars on the home market in 1946, Perry complained that this was a poor return on the reported £4.5 million surplus on revenues from motor vehicle duties. Moreover, despite the huge demand for cars, those who were fortunate enough to be able to take delivery of a new car had to covenant not to sell it for 12 months, and this created an inevitable black market in both new and secondhand cars.

Difficulties abounded: in the bitter winter of 1946–47, Sir Rowland Smith complained to Dearborn: 'It's bad enough to have the country frozen up, but the chaotic situation brought about by coal shortages, closing everybody down, is too serious for words. Despite Government regulations on the uses of coal and electricity, we are managing to work a shortened week. We are bloody but unbowed.'

Despite rising costs, Perry froze Ford prices, the only one of the major British manufacturers to follow this route. He commented: 'Ford has always applied the principle that higher wages and higher standards of living for all depend on lower costs and lower selling prices through increasingly large scale production.'

The 1945 Prefect was little changed from the pre-war model, but in car-hungry Britain, that didn't matter. What counted was getting your name on the waiting list for one!

John Wilmot, Minister of Supply in the Attlee Labour government, drives Ford's millionth vehicle, a 10hp Prefect, out of the factory with Sir Percival Perry in the passenger seat.

Placed in charge of maintaining this policy was Dagenham's rising star, Sir Patrick Hennessy, who was now general manager, with a seat on the board since 1945.

The first post-war cars were just revived pre-war models – Dagenham revived the old Anglia and Prefect virtually unchanged – but the first new Ford to appear after the Armistice was hardly in accord with the spirit of the austerity age. A streamlined 14.9hp saloon had been planned, but that never got past the mock-up stage, so the first new post-war Ford design, the Pilot, was a hefty V8 saloon. In fact, the Pilot was not as new as it seemed, for its body had already been used on the 1936 22hp V8, but it was made to look more imposing by a new bonnet and radiator shell designed by Dagenham's Australian chief body engineer Don Ward.

New look: but only for the lady. The interior of the post-war Anglia, with the art deco Bakelite 'instrument board' of the 1940 De Luxe model, was straight out of the late 1930s styling book.

A new 2.5-litre V8 engine had been developed from the 3.6-litre V8 which had served so valiantly during the war (and was still being installed in the company's 'utility cars'), for the Pilot. The new Ford was unveiled to the press on 14 August 1947 in the Rembrandt Hotel, South Kensington, known to many car enthusiasts as the venue for a series of wartime meetings which kept the flame of sporting motoring alive when pleasure motoring was 'on hold' for the duration of hostilities.

Around 125 journalists attended the launch, for the sight of any new car was exciting in those grey post-war days, though the weekly *Autocar*, which appeared the next day, had obviously had a privileged peek behind the scenes well in advance, for its four-page report included a fine cutaway drawing by the magazine's brilliant chief artist Max Millar, as well as detailed sketches of many constructional details.

Ford dealers got their chance to see the Pilot on 15 August, when six Pilots were parked in front of the clubhouse at the Stoke Poges Golf Club during the *Ford Times* Golf Tournament.

The retiring editor of the *Ford Times*, Edgar Duffield, was an old friend of Perry's with a genius for hyperbole, and he wrote his final article with gusto, claiming that 'if Dagenham could produce 500,000 V8 Pilots during the 12 months from 15 August 1947, those half-million of the new 2.5-litre V8 Pilot would be sold hands down long before they could be delivered'.

Sadly, it was not to be. The new engine was a disaster. In those days Ford lacked a test track, and the Motor Industry Research Association test facility in the Midlands was still in the future, so Ford used to carry out tests of its new models at night along the A13 Southend arterial road. One of the test drivers, Stan Paice, told the author in the 1970s that 'the 2.5-litre engine was totally gutless.' A rapid decision was taken to ditch the unsatisfactory power unit before any of the new model reached the public, in favour of the proven 3.6-litre unit. That was bad

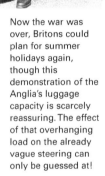

Now the war was over, Britons could plan for summer holidays again, though this demonstration of the Anglia's luggage capacity is scarcely reassuring. The effect of that overhanging load on the already vague steering can only be guessed at!

news in 1947, when the costly and restrictive horsepower tax still applied, but from January 1948 a new flat-rate £10 tax was imposed – on new cars only – to encourage British manufacturers to design larger-engined cars more suited to export markets.

Of course, there was still the matter of strict petrol rationing – in the week of the Pilot's launch, the government announced 10 per cent cuts in the allowances for 'essential' and 'semi-essential' car use, with the ordinary motorist faced with a reduction in his allowance to 1 gallon instead of 1.5 per petrol coupon. Still, at a basic price of £585 (plus purchase tax of £163), the Pilot was comfortably within the £1,000

The crown prince inspects his kingdom: in September 1945 Henry Ford was reluctantly persuaded to hand over power to his 28-year-old grandson Henry Ford II. Together they inspect a model of Ford's giant Rouge Plant in Detroit.

The American motor industry celebrated its Golden Jubilee in 1946. Here Henry and Clara Ford are reunited with old Henry's first car, the 1896 Quadricycle, under the watchful eye of grandson Henry Ford II. Does he realise grandfather's horseless carriage has no brakes?

limit at which the government imposed double purchase tax on the luxury car trade. The privileged few – like doctors and farmers – who could obtain supplementary petrol rations in those dismal days under the lack-lustre Attlee government, were ardent Pilot purchasers and over 22,000 were built before the model ceased production in car form in 1951 (though that fell a very long way short of Duffield's predicted half-million a year!).

While the government raised the ceiling on domestic vehicle sales in 1947, it was a futile quid pro quo for increasingly unrealistic (and unachievable) export targets of 80 per cent of car production, 65 per cent of commercials and 50 per cent of tractors.

In fact, the Society of Motor Manufacturers & Traders noted, 'The wretched conditions on the home market for cars continued to worsen as more and more vehicles were switched to the ports to intensify the national drive for exports. Registration figures for 1947 disclose that apart from nearly 7,500 ex-WD cars, only 142,000 cars came on the roads in the United Kingdom, as against an average annual consumption for the three years prior to the war of 303,000.'

Nevertheless, Dagenham still had confidence in the future, and in 1947 Ford-Britain took over the Kelsey-Hayes Wheel Company, which had been making wheels and brake drums for Ford at Dagenham since 1932. Extra production space was acquired at Walthamstow and a new engineering drawing office and development division was established in a factory at Rainham. Two years later a wartime aircraft factory at Langley, near Slough, which had built Hurricane fighters for the RAF (incidentally using Ford-built Merlin aeroengines) was taken over as a bulk storage facility which also made spare parts.

Those were desperate days: during the severe winter of 1946–47 a fuel crisis threatened to close down the Leamington factory, which had readily switched from making tank tracks to producing ploughs and cultivators for Britain's farmers – literally turning swords into ploughshares. Ford scoured the country for electrical generating equipment and located three 50-ton diesel generating sets on an army dump some 30 miles from the Leamington plant, which were installed over a weekend and were providing a 1500 kW electricity supply seven days after they had been found.

In 1948 Ford took the sales lead in Britain for the first time since the days of the Model T, though it was impossible to determine this from the official statistics published by the Society of Motor Manufacturers & Traders, which were a masterpiece of obfuscation that made it impossible to determine how many cars and trucks each company had built. Ford's lead was short-lived: in 1952 its two main rivals Austin and Morris merged to form the British Motor Corporation, which consequently became Britain's biggest motor manufacturer (although Ford remained noticeably more profitable).

A curious feature of Ford's 1948 versions of the Anglia and Prefect, announced at

After landing in the Brazilian port of Santos, these 1947 Anglias were assembled in the docks at the rate of nine cars a day by a seven-man team, then driven some 200 miles south-west over a 2600ft pass through the Serra de Santos mountains to the town of Curitaba.

The shape of things that never came: this was a proposal by Briggs for a post-war 14.9hp Ford model that never saw the light of day.

the October 1948 Earls Court Motor Show, was that they differed so little from the pre-war designs they displaced. Changes were merely cosmetic, with the Prefect gaining a more imposing radiator grille and front wings with inset headlamps, while the little Anglia actually reverted from the square-cut lines launched for 1940 to the more rounded front end – still with free-standing headlamps – of the 1937 '7Y' model that Pat Hennessy had taken to Dearborn. It only differed from the pre-war design in having twin grille apertures and a small protruding luggage boot, although for export markets where there was no tax on engine size, the Anglia was fitted with the more powerful 1172cc engine of the Prefect.

Ford's valiant attempts to sell the little Anglia and Prefect models on the American market, to which they had little relevance, were coordinated from an office in New York's Grand Central Station by sales executive Herbert Mortimore. The cars had a certain novelty value, but that was all. Despite Ford's optimistic statement that the Anglia 'proved to be the answer to the American family man's prayers – used to bigger cars at much bigger prices, the Anglia, which retailed at under $1,000 in America, was the car he was looking for', only 3,223 Dagenham-built Ford cars were registered in the whole of the US in 1948, representing about one percentage point of the parent Ford company's domestic sales. In contrast, America's Crosley, a home-grown small car, sold 25,400.

Mortimore had to work hard for even those sales, travelling widely across the States. In Corpus Christi, Texas, the assembled dealers told him that he stood no chance with his British cars, but then, fascinated by the way the stoutly-built

Englishman took snuff off the back of his hand ('This is the way Churchill takes snuff,' he assured them), they melted, and by the time the meeting closed, Mortimore had taken orders for over 200 cars.

Trucks were still an important part of Dagenham's output, and in 1948 the first all-British-designed Ford lorry, the ET6 Thames, made its debut. It was, however, still powered by the pre-war 3.6-litre V8 engine. In 1949, Dagenham's engineering department was split into separate passenger car and commercial vehicle divisions, each with its own executive engineer. The truck division, working toward a new range of trucks with a Dagenham-designed power unit, built two 6-ton prototypes in 1950. These would serve as the basis for both a new four-wheel-drive military chassis with a Canadian-built 3.9-litre V8 engine, and the forward control Thames Trader range to be launched in 1957, powered by Ford's own 'Cost Cutter' diesel and petrol engines, which had supplanted the thirsty V8 in 1953. With Trader production soon running at 100 units a day alongside the older ET6 range, Dagenham was stretched to bursting point, and truck production was transferred to the former parts depot at Langley in Buckinghamshire in 1961, ending over 30 years of heavy truck manufacture at Dagenham, which in 1959 recorded the building of its millionth commercial vehicle.

There had been a new figure at the helm in Dearborn since 1943, though not entirely from choice. Old Henry Ford was in his eightieth year and had become increasingly unpredictable. His naturally mercurial behaviour had been affected by a series of strokes, yet he obstinately refused to hand over to his son Edsel, instead relying increasingly on the dubious counsel of a former prizefighter named Harry Bennett, who ran Ford's strongarm security operations and had undoubted underworld connections.

For some perverse reason, Old Henry thought that his gentle, civilised son – who had been the guiding influence behind the most successful Ford models of the 1930s – was too soft, and consequently the streetwise,

'Conforming in full measure to the newspaper reporters' Hollywood-induced idea of the young American executive in an easy-fitting light grey suit", young Henry Ford II *(second from left)* came to Europe in 1948 with former General Motors executive Graeme Howard *(right)* as his right-hand man.

uncultured Bennett became the most powerful man in Dearborn.

Increasingly unhappy and frustrated, Edsel succumbed to cancer in 1943 – he was only 49 – and there was a very real threat that Harry Bennett would become the heir-apparent to the Ford Motor Company in his stead. Indeed, he claimed to have a codicil to Henry Ford's will that would put the company under the control of a board of trustees headed by Bennett. Meanwhile, Henry announced that he was taking over the presidency of the Ford Motor Company. As Dearborn floundered, the American government worried that a company vital to the American war effort was in peril of slipping into anarchy, and plucked Henry Ford's 25-year-old grandson

The Ford-Britain directors meet in the company's 88 Regent Street boardroom in 1949. Lord Perry *(fourth from left)* had resigned as chairman in 1948, though he remained a director. Sir Patrick Hennessy and Sir Rowland Smith, the duo who would guide Dagenham through the 1950s, flank him. Lord Airedale *(head of table)* took over as caretaker chairman from Perry and was succeeded by Rowland Smith in 1950. Lord Airedale's neighbour with the Mephistophelean smile is Graeme Howard, representing the newly-founded Ford International Division: next to him is Sir Stanford Cooper, Ford-Britain's vice-chairman and board member of Ford International. New boy Viscount Portal KG, Marshal of the Royal Air Force and Controller of Atomic Energy in the Ministry of Supply, one of a number of public figures and eminent businessmen on the Ford board, sits on the left.

Henry II out of the US Navy to save the situation.

While Henry Ford II admitted he was 'green, and looking for answers', he had been keeping a close watch on the company's production figures while he was in the Navy and had already realised that the company was in need of young, smart, college-educated management to face the challenges of the post-war market.

He had an idea of the size of that market, too: 'I think that a second car in the American garage is not an impossible hope,' he remarked. 'It cannot be a European midget and it cannot be a piece of stripped down transportation. But it could be a considerably smaller car, provided it has all the present comforts and engineering and can be made for a price considerably below the price of the pre-war Ford.'

Elected a vice-president in December 1943, young Henry was clearly the heir apparent, but the management of the company was fragmented. 'Cast Iron' Charlie Sorensen, for so long Old Henry's strong man, was ousted, along with engineer Laurence Sheldrick and 'Bob' Gregorie. All had played a part in creating the Model Y, the little car that had saved Dagenham (Gregorie, though, was re-hired in 1944).

Ford's rivals likened the management ladder at Ford to the Indian rope trick – an executive would climb and climb to the top and disappear.

Although the upper echelons of Ford were divided into Henry II and Harry

Bennett factions, and although the administration of the company was, at times, eccentric in the extreme ('In one department,' said a bemused Henry Ford II, 'they figured their costs by weighing the pile of invoices on a scale!') the company carried on as though nothing had happened.

Indeed, *Fortune* magazine remarked in 1944, that apart from a few minor setbacks, 'Ford has met and surpassed schedules. Barring some colossal folly involving labour, production for war should be almost automatic from now on.'

Young Henry met dealers, planned for the future, and authorised changes to the design of the post-war cars that were already on the drawing board.

His grandfather's powers were now visibly waning, even though that 1944 *Fortune* article praised Old Henry's 'zest for life… he dips his comb in salt water for the health of his hair… he wears peculiar, very sensible shoes. The uppers consist of narrow strips of leather woven in and out…'

It all came to a head in September 1945, when Henry Ford's wife Clara and Edsel's widow Eleanor persuaded the stubborn old man to stand down in favour of his grandson.

The end for Bennett came swiftly: once Henry II had been voted president, the man who would be king had no future. With a snarled 'You're taking over a billion dollar organisation here that you haven't contributed a thing to!' Bennett left the room. As the momentous meeting drew to a close, Henry II strode after him. The two men were alone a while: when Henry II came back, Bennett's career was over. He was gone in a week. The new president had much to do in Dearborn: the rest of his empire could wait. It was in capable hands.

In fact, it was Dagenham that was charged with getting Ford-Germany back on an even keel. Built among fields on the outskirts of Cologne and hidden by the smoke screen which also hid the neighbouring Badische Anilin chemical works, Ford-Germany's factory had suffered little damage from the air-raids which had virtually destroyed the centre of the city.

It had suffered more from German artillery as the Germans fell back across the Rhine at the beginning of March 1945. Convinced that Allied troops were sheltering in the Ford plant, the 'Kamikaze Wehrmacht' shelled it over a five-week period, blowing out the windows, destroying the test and repair shops and damaging office buildings. However, little damage was done to the production machinery, and in mid-April American military police occupied the plant, and repair work was put in hand.

At the end of the war, the German authorities had given instructions for production machinery which had been moved to 'dispersal factories' to be blown up to prevent it from falling into Allied hands, but the employees of Ford-Werke had disobeyed orders. All that remained was to get the machinery back into the factory, where its mounts and power connections were ready to receive it.

The Supreme Headquarters of the Allied Expeditionary Force (SHAEF) asked for a team from Dagenham to go to Cologne as soon as it was practicable to resume production.

The three-man SHAEF team, headed by Dagenham manager Charles Thacker,

A fleet (or flight?) of Ford Pilots for the Kenyan police in 1949. Pilots fitted with special aluminium 'safari' bodies were also used by the wardens in Kenya's Nairobi National Park.

reached Cologne in May 1945. Although the plant management had told the Americans that it would take six weeks to get back into production, Thacker took no notice. He simply applied Dagenham methods to the problem, and the first post-war truck – assembled from components on hand – left the plant on VE Day, 8 May 1945, watched by Thacker and his two assistants.

Money was short – nearly 1.4 million reichsmarks kept in a safe stored in an air raid shelter had gone missing in the confused days at the end of the war – and the adverse exchange rate meant that exports could only be made at a considerable loss.

Nevertheless, by guile and barter – two trucks for 100 bicycles so that workers could ride to the factory, three tons of potatoes for a chassis and cab so that workers could eat, chassis in exchange for chipboard to make cabs – the Dagenham men got Cologne back on its feet.

Other Dagenham managers helped put other European companies back on their feet. From Cologne, Charles Thacker was sent to Ford-Belgium as manager, and carried out a competent reorganisation of the company, even though he was 'not familiar with the language, customs, tradition and history of the country' – not such a handicap as it might seem, for throughout the Ford empire the *lingua franca* of management was English. Allen Barke, a future managing director of Ford-Britain, encountered the real-life Harry Limes of the post-war black market in Austria while tracing missing production machinery that had been 'liberated' from the old Ford-Hungary plant in Budapest. It was not until 1948, a year after the death of his 83-year-old grandfather from a cerebral haemorrhage, that Henry Ford II felt that he had time to come and look at his European inheritance.

Accompanied by a spare, charming former General Motors vice-president named Graeme K. Howard, recently appointed a consultant on international affairs to Ford, Henry Ford II and his wife Anne arrived in Southampton aboard the *Queen Mary* on Tuesday 10 February. It had been a stormy passage across the Atlantic, cutting short the young Fords' budding careers as champion deck quoits players.

This had left Anne Ford time to make friends with another passenger, film star Merle Oberon, and the two women came down the gangway arm-in-arm as young Henry waved cheerfully at the crowds gathered on the quayside.

The directors of Ford-Britain had sent a brand-new V8 Pilot, the flagship of their fleet, to carry the Fords up to London, even though young Henry had condemned the introduction of this essentially pre-war design as 'a lot of nonsense'.

Ford's dislike of the Pilot was revealed when he axed a proposed new model, a re-bodied Pilot built on dies bought from Humber and scheduled to be unveiled at that October's London Motor Show. He dismissed the new-look Pilot as 'a product-rigged affair... this bastard interim product'.

It was perhaps an unfair criticism, for the British automotive industry was hamstrung by the manifold restrictions imposed by the socialist government of the colourless Clement Attlee. And was it worth developing new designs when private motorists faced an indefinite wait to buy new cars – a government white paper had assessed the home market at 50,000 cars 'for essential users' – and then were prevented from using them by the withdrawal at the end of 1947 of the basic petrol ration to save dollars?

Though this was his first visit to England since taking control of the Ford empire,

During 1948, Dagenham exported 12,250 10hp cars and vans to the United States, including this order for the salesmen of 'Nutty Club' candies, which underlines the fact that many Americans bought the little Fords for their novelty value.

The Ford Prefect was restyled in 1948, with larger front wings with inbuilt headlamps. This American customer looks pleased with his purchase.

Henry II had already learned much. Engineering, he suggested, was the weak point of the British Ford organisation: 'A chief engineer is required as well as a body and styling engineer… Action is necessary!'

He lost no time in making his presence felt, 'speeding toward a series of engagements that would have daunted the majority of men'. His first appointment was with the BBC, where he recorded an interview for that evening's mass-audience *Light Programme* news summary *Radio Newsreel*.

Then, flanked by Smith, Hennessy and Cooper, he held a press conference in the Savoy Hotel, attended by 400 journalists. With only a minimum of notes, he handled the meeting with cheerful confidence. 'He looked,' said one candid reporter, 'like an ex-football player who has put on weight (which is what he is)…'

Henry Ford's grasp of the British situation was precise: 'Over the next six months,' he told the assembled pressmen, 'Dagenham plans to export 6,000 cars – worth in total approximately $4.5 million – to the United States. Moreover, 1947 was Ford-Britain's best-yet production year, with 114,872 vehicles built, beating the previous record year of 1937 by over 1,000 vehicles.

'In January this year, Dagenham workers broke all previous records by producing 7,200 vehicles – including tractors – for overseas markets. We believe that this makes the British Ford company the largest exporters in the British motor industry.'

Then, having reeled off his set statement, he leaned back in an armchair to face a barrage of questions. The first one was obviously meant to catch him off guard: 'What do you think of history?' queried a journalist, obviously thinking of old Henry Ford's frequently misquoted remark that 'history is bunk'.

Dagenham's publicity people haunted Britain's film studios in the late 1940s, for the combination of cars and stars was an irresistible one. Here *Two Cities* starlet Lana Morris, fresh from playing 'Bouncie Barrington' in the Technicolor comedy *Trottie True*, gives some unconvincing cosmetic attention to a 1949 Prefect.

Lord Perry in
retirement.
Increasingly troubled
by colitis, Perry spent
much time in the
Bahamas for his
health and died there
in 1956.

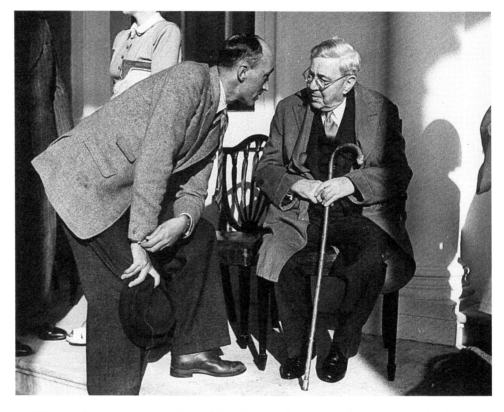

'History is a very interesting subject,' parried Henry, who was to make his own brand of history in the years to come.

He then dealt skilfully with questions on topics ranging from agricultural machinery to diesel engines, from the potential demand for British cars in the States ('terrific') to forward spending plans. The young man searching for answers had obviously found quite a few of them already.

And he was honest enough to admit when he hadn't. 'Can you tell us the cash value of the concerns that you control?' asked a journalist.

'No,' said the candid young Ford. 'I haven't the slightest idea!'

The following morning, he visited Dagenham and drove its 250,000th post-war vehicle – a left-hand drive 10hp Prefect destined for the United States – off the production line. The antique charm of Ford's British products failed to impress Henry, who was to declare: 'In respect of English cars, I would say that I myself do not like them.'

Nevertheless, as he stepped from the Prefect, 'good old Henry' was mobbed by cheering Dagenham workers anxious to shake his hand. He was to reciprocate by sending a $5 food parcel to every worker at Dagenham to relieve the tedium of food rationing.

Watching the enthusiastic welcome the Dagenham men gave to their big boss, 'It's the most spontaneous thing I've seen since the Royal Wedding,' enthused an American newspaperman who had reported the wedding of Princess Elizabeth in Westminster Abbey three months earlier.

On a post-war visit to the University of New Brunswick in Canada, Sir Patrick Hennessy *(front, left)* introduces Henry Ford II *(front, right)* to his wartime boss and the university's benefactor, Lord Beaverbrook *(front, centre)*.

Then Henry Ford II was driven quickly back into London for lunch with the British Ford dealers at the Savoy.

'It's the first time I've ever addressed dealers outside the USA,' he told them, 'so I'm not going to tell you what to do because you know that better than I do... but to overcome competition, we need teamwork, and I'm putting you first in that team because you have personal contact with the public, and you know what the public wants. It doesn't matter how good the products happen to be – they're no good unless the dealers are behind them... but I'm sure you'll agree that we have to modernise our British products – and we've got to do it quickly!

'It has always been Ford policy to produce in the greatest quantity possible and to encourage the largest possible distribution.

'Our factory at Dagenham is an expression of this policy.'

That evening at Claridge's Henry Ford met the leaders of the British motor industry, the editors of the Fleet Street newspapers and government officials. In a half-hour speech, he discussed the employment situation in America, where for the first time over 60 million were in work, with an annual disposable dollar income worth £43,500 million. He analysed public attitudes to the newly-formed United Nations and Soviet Russia and the Communist threat, and outlined Ford plans for the future.

In contrast, the response by the socialist Minister of Supply, George Strauss, rang

In Britain to film *Edward my Son* with Deborah Kerr for MGM in 1949, Spencer Tracy was yet another film star hijacked by Dagenham's publicity department to pose with a Ford, this time a V8 Pilot. However, the reflections in the hubcap suggest this may have been a skilful montage.

somewhat hollow. Congratulating Ford on its wartime tractor production and export achievements, Strauss claimed that 'Britain led the world' in motor cycles, small cars, small diesel engines and jet engines and topped it with the uninspiring statistic that Britain was the world's largest exporter of pedal cycles.

One vital task that had to be achieved during Henry Ford's visit to England was the freeing of the managerial log-jam at Dagenham. Although he was close to his 70th birthday and in failing health, Lord Perry was clinging on to power despite an increasing inability to attend board meetings.

For some months he had been abroad at his holiday home in the Bahamas and his

Unveiling this statue of Henry Ford by sculptor Dyson-Smith in front of Dagenham's office block on 14 October 1948, Lord Airedale remarked that it was 'an inspiration to all who pass by'. Shop floor worker J. Swan, 21 years with the company, paid tribute to Henry Ford as 'a great mechanic'.

place had been taken at Ford-Britain's monthly board meetings by his deputy, Lord Airedale, an affable, monocled old nobleman of 68 who was a director of the Bank of England. It was vital to the future of Ford at Dagenham that Perry should step aside to make room for the management team of Smith and Hennessy on whom Detroit was pinning its hopes for the future.

On 18 February, as the Ford party prepared to fly to meet the Ford-France directors in Paris aboard their chartered DC-3 airliner *Clipper Line Yankee*, Perry turned 70. It was the excuse Henry II needed to start the management shake-up that was needed for the new post-war world. Perry was probably summoned to England immediately: he was certainly present to chair the company's Annual General Meeting in mid-April. Unusually, Airedale represented the Dearborn directors, a role customarily assumed by the Chairman of Ford-Britain.

After conducting the main business of the meeting, Perry dropped his bombshell by announcing 'I am resigning as Chairman,' though it was not clear whether he was resigning voluntarily or because he had been ordered to. Certainly the impression Dagenham management got was that he had been pushed.

Airedale took over as 'caretaker' Chairman while a thorough reorganisation of Ford-Britain was set in motion, 'from the Chairman down to and including the most junior executive'. Rowland Smith became Deputy Chairman, Stanford Cooper Vice Chairman with additional responsibility for the 'European Associated Companies' and Patrick Hennessy was made General Manager.

Henry Ford II, recently voted 'Man of the Year' in America, and his right-hand man Ernest Breech came to London to confer with the new triumvirate, with whom

The 'dynamically ruthless' Charles Sorensen *(left)* meets his old sparring partner Pat Hennessy *(second from left)* after the war. While Hennessy's star kept rising – he became Chairman of Ford-Britain in 1956 – Sorensen fell from grace in 1943 after serving old Henry Ford for 40 years.

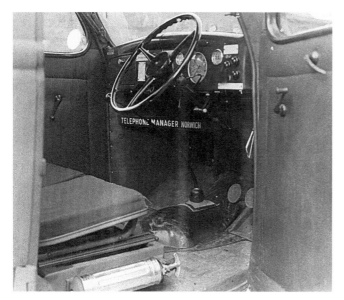

The utilitarian interior of a 1940s Ford V8 telephone van has all the uncomfortable hallmarks of Austerity Britain.

the company made £57,000 agreements securing their exclusive services for the company 'over a number of years'.

Henry Ford II wrote some perceptive character portraits of his new British board in his diary. Airedale, he thought 'a happy choice… he has the attributes and character of those men who made English history'. Smith, who would succeed him in the short term, was 'a man with an uncommon lot of horse-sense, integrity and ability to handle and get along with people'.

The punctilious Stanford Cooper was 'charged with working out the best financial and legal mechanism' for Ford-Britain to transfer its associated European companies (apart from Cork) to the direct control of Dearborn. In June 1948 managers from Ford companies all around the world were summoned to Dearborn to be told by Henry Ford II that a new Ford-International Division was to be formed to replace the 'preposterous' state of affairs that had reigned in Ford's overseas companies: 'This is an American company and it's going to be run from America,' he stated. In January 1949, a press release announced the formation of Ford-International

Ken Wharton and Joy Cooke, famed for their rallying high jinks, pose with the impressive bonnet-full of trophies they were awarded when they won the 1949 Tulip Rally outright. Wharton was to win three Tulip Rallies for Ford to gain the Dutch event's Silver Tulip Challenge Trophy.

Inc, which became operational at the end of April.

The scheme under which Ford in Dearborn bought the shares in the Associated Companies for £4.3 million was a masterpiece of accountancy which provided returns to American and British shareholders and gave cash rather than shares to Ford-America to avoid exposure to capital appreciation tax. It showed that Henry Ford II's faith in Stanford Cooper's financial skills had not been misplaced.

However, Hennessy was 'the executive upon whom we hope to build the future Dagenham. He has all the potential qualities which the position of either Managing Director or Board Chairman demand. He will be rounded out and developed by his association and experience with Lord Airedale, Sir Rowland Smith and Sir Stanford Cooper over the immediate years.

'We must, however,' concluded Henry, 'look ahead and see that Sir Patrick Hennessy is supported by two or even three executive assistants who have the potential qualifications for Assistant Managing Director, and ultimately Managing Director when Sir Patrick Hennessy moves up to the chief executive post of Board Chairman.'

Against the backdrop of Lower Manhattan, a 1948 export Anglia crosses Brooklyn Bridge. This American version of the Anglia had a unique three-panel radiator grill and the more powerful 1172cc engine of the Prefect.

Restored by Ford apprentices in the mid-1980s, the late King George VI's last car, a 1951 Garner-bodied V8 Pilot shooting brake is now in the Royal Motor Museum at Sandringham. The Queen Mother once helped chauffeur Harold Fishburn perform an engine change at Balmoral!

Chapter Seven

NEW MODELS, NEW POLICIES

HAND-IN-HAND with this managerial reorganisation came a revitalisation of the company's planned products, for the obsolescent range then leaving the Dagenham production lines looked increasingly dated and offered little for style-conscious export markets like the US.

At the time of his visit, Henry Ford II had summed up the situation succinctly: 'Our English company at this juncture is the most important operation in our international scheme of things. We desperately need an English small car export source.

'The styling of the products must be modernised and made universally acceptable, and their costs must be appreciably reduced. Consequently the organisation should have priority of attention.

'Finally, the organisation needs assistance and encouragement, and appreciation of their difficulties and a recognition of the job done under conditions of extraordinary obstacles. Carping, unconstructive criticism will butter no parsnips. Encouragement and help is what is needed.'

The key factor in shaping the first all-new designs to be produced by Dagenham since the 1930s was the Attlee government's 1947 budget, which swept away the long outdated and discredited horsepower tax and replaced it with a flat rate £10 duty (although this new measure only applied to new cars, and owners of large-engined second-hand cars still had to pay the old exorbitant road tax).

This meant that British manufacturers could now use modern large-bore, short-stroke engines to appeal to export markets without penalising their home market customers. Of course, with the naiveté typical of politicians with no experience of industry, the government obviously expected these new power units to come into use immediately, whereas of course the design, tooling and manufacturing necessary to put a new engine into production required several years and a large investment.

Hennessy summed up the government's stultifying policy succinctly when he visited Dearborn in June 1948: 'They tell us what to do, what to make, when to make it and what to do with it when we have made it... Government Socialist Planning means this: on the first of January they tell us what sheet metal we are going to get for January, February and March. In some cases we fabricated the steel

These are early prototypes of the four-cylinder Consul (*left*) and six-cylinder Zephyr, registered in June 1950 and photographed on the gravel drive of Perry's Essex home, Stock Hall. Actual production of the Consul did not begin until 1 January 1951, while the first production Zephyr left the Dagenham lines on 12 February.

for January, February and March six months before the beginning of the period. In some cases we have to start on things a year or 15 months ahead of production. They tell us the day before, and they call that planning…'

One important piece of planning to be undertaken by the newly-instituted Dagenham Policy Committee, which had met for the first time in January 1948, was the design of a new range of family cars responding to the new road tax regime. The attitude of Dagenham's top management was stated in an article in *The Times*: 'These men believe that Britain should not attempt to copy the vehicles of other countries and that she should develop a new and completely distinctive style of her own. Moreover, they believe that so long as the most economical form of motoring is required (as it always will be in many parts of the world) it is the business of Ford, Dagenham, to supply that need. In its view it is Dagenham's task to set the standard of low price and value for the money. Nevertheless they stipulate that the cars they make must take four people safely and comfortably as well as economically.'

Ford's role in the government-inspired export drive was an important one, particularly following the 30 per cent devaluation of the pound in September 1949. The Attlee government then set a ceiling of 110,000 units on the home market; Dagenham's waiting list was for more than 275,000 cars!

Nevertheless, planning for the day when the compulsory export quotas would be swept away – though that that happy day was long in coming – was essential, and while the lower prices created by devaluation gave the essentially pre-war Dagenham

The most famous Zephyr Six was the left-hand drive 'VHK 194', rallied extensively by Dutch driver Maurice Gatsonides. His co-driver Peter Worledge got the job because he worked for Cape Asbestos, who provided the special brake and clutch linings for the car!

products a temporary attractiveness, something more suited to the changed conditions of the post-war world was urgently needed.

Since Ford still lacked a sufficiently large engineering department, Hennessy approached the Treasury seeking clearance for the necessary dollar allocation to enable Dagenham to pay Dearborn the requisite service fees to buy American engineering assistance. Dagenham's export activities fully justified the request, and subsequently Treasury official Sir Herbert Britain informed Airedale and Hennessy that the Government was prepared to provide up to $4.5 million to pay for American machinery and equipment.

A small delegation of Dagenham engineers, headed by executive engineer George Halford, was sent to Dearborn to work with their American colleagues on the new British range. Accompanying Halford were Fred Hart, who would play a key role in shaping the new products of the 1960s, and Briggs body engineer Andy Cox, whose body design night classes organised at Dagenham in the 1940s and 1950s were the foundation of an independent British styling department.

While the new models had some family resemblance to the style-setting '49 Fords designed by the flamboyant stylist George Walker – an industrial designer brought in as an outside consultant, precipitating Bob Gregorie's second departure from Ford –

which had given the American company a refreshing new image, technically they were streets ahead of the Dearborn product and broke much new ground for Ford worldwide.

Exactly who was responsible for the design of the new British Fords is not clear. In charge of Dearborn engineering since 1946 was Harold T. Youngren, formerly with Oldsmobile and Borg-Warner. Though he and an assistant named John Oswald did spend time in Dagenham, Youngren had certainly shown little spark of originality in the chassis engineering of the '49ers, with their separate frame and body construction and flat-head V8 power units.

In comparison, Dagenham's new models – 'one of the outstanding attractions' of the 1950 London Motor Show, where Princess Margaret was shown the new models by Sir Rowland Smith – were true 'clean sheet of paper' designs which inherited nothing from previous models. For a start, they had the Ford Motor Company's first monocoque bodies – the only precedent was the integral body/chassis construction of the 1935 Lincoln-Zephyr built by Briggs for Ford's upmarket stablemate, which was a sort of halfway bridge to a true load-carrying monocoque.

Ford promoted the spacious new models, which differed only in front end design and were badged 'Consul' (1.5-litre four-cylinder) and 'Zephyr' (2.2-litre six-cylinder), as the 'Five Star Cars' for their five main features: overhead valve engines – the Zephyr was Ford-Britain's first-ever six-cylinder model – with oversquare cylinder dimensions to take full advantage of the new tax regime; monocoque bodywork; independent front suspension (another 'first' for Ford-Britain), hydraulic brakes on all four wheels and 'centre-slung' seating within the wheelbase for a comfortable ride.

Pendant pedals and 12-volt electrics were also new for a Ford car. The 13-inch wheels were the smallest yet seen on a British car of that size, there were press-button rotary door latches and the clutch was hydraulically operated.

In hindsight, although the new cars led the British market in many respects (but annoyingly still had three-speed transmissions and vacuum-operated windscreen wipers), their most important feature was the independent front suspension, a completely new system devised by Ford of America's vice-president of engineering, Earle S. MacPherson. This had long hollow king pins that acted as the cylinders of hydraulic dampers and also carried a cup that supported a coil spring which bore the weight of the car. A novelty then, this 'MacPherson Strut' suspension has since become an industry standard used on cars the world over. The production machinery instal-led at Dagenham to produce

Triumphant return: Gatsonides *(left)* and Worledge bring 'VHK 194' home aboard a Bristol Freighter of Silver City Airways' Channel Air Bridge after their victory in the 1953 Monte Carlo Rally. The shield over the radiator was to cut down back glare from the foglights.

the new Consul and Zephyr broke new ground, too, with automatic transfer machinery doubling output of cylinder blocks.

Dagenham managed the changeover from the old models to the new, with their radically different technology, with remarkable ease. Although output from the old production lines in the first half of 1950 had been a factory record of almost 110,000 units, the change-over took place during the summer holiday shutdown and none of the workers needed to be put on short time or laid off.

Remarkably, there were few of the teething troubles that might have been expected with such a radically new design, though early examples suffered sufficiently from noisy back axles for Zephyr production to be halted while a cure was found, and the monocoque bodyshell proved remarkably strong. The new cars were lively performers, a fact vividly demonstrated in 1953 when Dutchman Maurice Gatsonides won the Monte Carlo Rally driving a virtually-standard Zephyr Six. One ingenious feature was a switch in the brake-light circuit so that 'Gatso' could fool less skilful competitors following too close on his tail into braking far too late on bends.

Initially, the Consul and Zephyr were only available as four-door saloons, but a prototype Zephyr Six two-door convertible was displayed at the October 1951 Motor Show. However, problems with structural rigidity meant that the convertible versions of the Consul and Zephyr did not reach full production until 1953. These were not built by Briggs but modified and trimmed in the Coventry works of Carbodies, a company founded by one Bobby Jones in 1919 to specialise in 'contract' building of special bodywork for mass-producers, which had recently become part of the BSA group. Production convertibles needed a special 'X'-form bracing welded beneath the floor to prevent the bodyshell from cracking. An unusual feature was a hood that could be used in the 'coupé de ville' position; the Zephyr convertible's hood was electro-hydraulically operated.

Despite being built by an outside supplier, the convertible was classed as a production model since the trimmed bodies were returned to Dagenham for final assembly. Interestingly, more of the expensive Zephyr (4,048) were sold than of the cheaper Consul (3,749). This was in contrast to the output of the saloon versions of the Consul (231,481) and Zephyr (175,311). The figure for the Zephyr included 22,634 of a more powerful de luxe model, the Zephyr Zodiac, launched in 1953 with 'all the special fittings that the fonder owner loves', including heater and demister, screen washer, whitewall tyres, two-tone paint, leather upholstery and gold-plated insignia (though the radio was an extra).

Another outside bodybuilder who modified the Consul and Zephyr with Ford approval was E.D. Abbott of Farnham, whose 'luggage locker expansion' launched at the 1954 Motor Show used a special extended roof pressed out using concrete dies, an extra pair of side windows and a side-hinged rear door to create an estate car.

Alongside the glamorous new models, the old faithful Anglia and Prefect continued in production with reliability and low price their principal virtues.

One revolutionary new development to come from Dagenham during this period was Ford's first diesel engine, a personal project of Sir Patrick Hennessy's.

Dagenham engineers had begun work on a diesel power unit under his supervision as early as 1944, but the American directors, viewing the diesel from the security of a land awash with cheap gasoline, had little sympathy with the project. Hennessy argued his case with Sir Rowland Smith, who declared: 'I'm going to back you – you haven't been wrong in my time.'

The Americans declared that the diesel project 'would wreck the company,' but Hennessy stood firm. 'Let me have my way or fire me,' he declared. 'For some extraordinary reason they didn't fire me,' he recalled later.

One of the prime reasons for developing the new power unit was the Fordson tractor, and in 1951 Ford unveiled the Dagenham-developed 'New Fordson Major', another of Sir Patrick Hennessy's personal projects. The brief was simple: 'Design a new tractor based on past experience but embodying the latest refinements and engineering techniques. Three completely new engines are required, petrol, vaporising oil and diesel – but using basic common components.'

The development story of the new power unit revealed that Ford now had its own engine test facilities, with soundproof cells where engines could be 'run at maximum load, day in, day out'. Prototype tractors were tested on the company's own field test station adjoining the Dagenham factory and on farms in Norfolk and North Wales.

The Fordson Major was a huge success: in its first year £7 million-worth were ordered for the United States.

Alongside the tractor unit, a new four-cylinder truck engine was developed, with a petrol version appearing in 1953 and a diesel the following year. Lessons learned in the development of the truck engine were simultaneously applied to the tractor unit, with the vaporising oil version soon being withdrawn as this fuel had been supplanted by diesel. A six-cylinder truck engine followed, which was used in the new Thames Trader series of 1957, and in 1958 came a revised Power Major tractor.

The dynamometer cells were used for testing car engines, too: engines taken at random from the production lines were run in on the dynamometer for five-and-a-half hours before being accelerated to peak revolutions over a seven-hour period and then, after nine hours fuel consumption, power and torque readings were taken to ensure that the engine met the correct engineering specification.

However, in those days, not everything was left to the measuring devices: there was also a keen-eared technician with a stethoscope 'listening to the piston beat of the engine as it runs on the test bed'.

Bizarrely, the whole process of production at Dagenham, 'from raw materials to finished product' was synthesised and set to specially-commissioned music in a Ford-sponsored film entitled 'Opus 65', which premiered at the 1952 Edinburgh Film Festival. The music was by 35-year-old Royal College of Music graduate Richard Arnell, who had written his first film score for the celebrated documentary producer Robert Flaherty's *The Land* in 1941 and had his music performed under such distinguished conductors as Bernard Herrmann, Leopold Stokowski and Sir Thomas Beecham.

Though engineering now had its own base at Rainham, the building was far from perfect. It was an old building, and its roof was infested with sparrows, which regularly left their 'calling cards' on engineering drawings. Rainham's engineering director was a colourful American named Olly Schjolin who, exasperated by the rain of bird droppings, brought an airgun to work to cull the noisome sparrows.

A move to improve the situation came in 1952, when Ford bought a former glassworks in Lodge Road, Birmingham. This was a site which went back to the dawn of the industrial revolution, when one William Shakespeare had built a 'glass house' in the first decade of the 19th century alongside the canal branch that served the famed Soho Works of James Watt's partner Matthew Boulton. Glassmaking remained on the site until around 1950, when the then occupants, John Walsh Walsh, went into liquidation with new office buildings unfinished.

Ford completed the work and set up an engineering research centre. The reason for locating this so far from Dagenham was simple: the Midlands was then the epicentre of the British motor industry, and it was simpler to recruit automotive engineers there than anywhere else. Major component manufacturers were nearby, and although there were no on-site road-testing facilities – braking and handling tests were often carried out in the car park of a nearby pub – the MIRA testing grounds were only 20 miles away.

By now, Ford had its own testing ground, on a disused World War Two USAF airfield near the village of Matching Green in north-west Essex. Where in the closing stages of the war twin-engined Marauder bombers had taken off to attack Germany, a new small car was developed to replace the uncompromisingly upright Prefect.

When Dagenham had begun work on the new small car range, Hennessy went to Dearborn to see Henry Ford II, who informed him that 'the development work on this project is a matter for the Dagenham company's decision'. Hennessy – who thought it 'a tragic thing' that Dagenham's engineering staff was not really large enough for all the ambitious projects he had in mind – relished the British company's growing independence, and when a journalist asked whether Dagenham policy was 'strongly, partly or negligibly controlled by your American associates', was firmly assured that it was only 'partly controlled'.

For the new '100E' range, this meant that the cars were designed in England, though American stylists headed the Briggs Bodies team. One suggestion – 'Chavant' – looked amazingly like the Wolseley 1500 that went on the market in 1957, but the chosen design was basically designed by George Snyder from Briggs's Detroit studio, with the front and rear ends styled by Briton Colin Neale: Dearborn engineering vice-president Earle MacPherson 'made helpful suggestions'.

The 100E – produced in two-door Anglia and four-door Prefect versions – was Dagenham's second monocoque design and although it echoed the shape of its Consul

Codenamed 'Chavant', this full-size Plasticene mock-up was Dagenham's first proposal for the 100E, with a front end that seems to portend the shape of Wolseleys to come.

and Zephyr big sisters, and shared their MacPherson Strut independent suspension system, the engine was still a long-stroke sidevalve with a swept volume of 1172cc. Curiously, though, this was an entirely new unit.

The first 100E Anglia leaves the Dagenham production line on 28 October 1953.

What had happened was that, because of the cost of developing the Consul and Zephyr range, Dagenham was having to make economies. While it would have been nice to have developed a small overhead valve unit, Ford decided instead to create a new sidevalve engine that shared the same bore and stroke measurements so that the existing production machinery could be used.

It was the last sidevalve unit from a major manufacturer and, curiously, still had cast-in white metal bearings on the big ends and main bearings instead of the shell bearings that had become commonplace throughout the industry. Curiouser yet, Dagenham continued manufacturing the obsolescent Ford Ten engine alongside the new 100E unit, with which it had no component in common. The pre-war engine was used in the bottom-of-the-range Popular, billed as 'Britain's cheapest car', an even-fewer-frills version of the former export Anglia. This mechanised coelacanth, whose chassis retained the transverse leaf spring suspension layout of the 1908 Model T, remained in production until 1959.

Four hundred miles away in Cologne, Ford-Germany continued to turn out its version of the pre-war 1172cc Ten engine, used in the post-war Taunus, which bore

This is the 300E van variant of the 100E in its 7cwt version: the 5cwt van had horizontal louvres in its radiator grille and lighter rear springs.

a passing resemblance to the 100E range but was an entirely different car.

The former links between Ford's European companies had been well and truly broken by the war, and in fact in some Continental markets, Ford-Britain and Ford-Germany were keen rivals, developing entirely different models to meet the same basic specification and fighting for the same slice of the market. It was a bizarre situation.

Strangely, although the Ford Motor Company had been operating on the world stage virtually since its foundation in 1903, it had no formal co-ordinating body for its worldwide operations until after old Henry Ford ceded control to his grandson in 1945. Ford's International Division had been formed in September 1946, but although it represented a third of Ford sales, it seemed strangely reluctant to carry out a process of rationalisation to eliminate anomalies like the internal conflict between Dagenham and Cologne.

This policy – or rather, lack of one – led to the collapse and sale of Ford's manufacturing interests in France in 1954, for the Paris company had been trying to sell a rejected Dearborn design for a post-war small car for America – the 22hp V8 Vedette – on a market that had little need for anything but utilitarian small cars. To have developed such a car would have cost maybe $100 million (and led to a third strand in Ford's internal European rivalries). With the obvious answer staring them in the face, Ford perversely sold its modern, well-equipped factory at Poissy, west of Paris, to Simca (today, the Poissy site is a thriving Peugeot factory), and the Ford Vedette became a Simca.

'Nous avons été vendus comme le mouton,' lamented François Depasse, son of Ford's earliest Ford agent.

The only voice of sanity in the whole affair was that of Sir Patrick Hennessy, who forthrightly told Dearborn that 'Ford France could have been successful with good management'. Dearborn, for once, ignored his sage advice. And lived to regret it.

Facelift in Finchingfield: pictured in one of rural Essex's prettiest villages, the 1957 100E Anglia had a new 'lattice' grille and 'textured headlight mouldings'. A larger rear window was another change.

In January 1953, Dagenham built its two millionth vehicle – a Zephyr Six – which was driven off the production line by Sir Rowland Smith, just as he had driven the first vehicle away just over 21 years earlier.

Sir Rowland was soon able to report that during the first three months of 1953 one-third of all new cars registered had been built at Dagenham, and new coke ovens and a new commercial vehicle assembly building were fully operational. Dagenham was producing more Zephyrs and diesel tractors, as well building new army vehicles for the Government's rearmament programme. Smith could also claim that the blast furnace had produced a record 1,553,760 tons of iron between relinings and that the power house could now produce 44,000kW, against 10,000kW in 1934.

Nevertheless, Sir Patrick Hennessy was the real Dagenham power house: although he didn't actually succeed Sir Rowland Smith as Chairman of Ford-Britain until 1956, in practice he had held the job in all but name for years.

In 1953 he had taken the bold step of introducing the American discipline of product planning to the British motor industry. This had been one of the great changes introduced in Dearborn by Henry Ford II, who realised that the seat-of-the-pants methods of his grandfather no longer made sense, and that new models had to be tailored to the needs of the market.

Working as Hennessy's personal assistant was a bright young graduate named Terry Beckett, who had the unusual background of having qualified in both engineering and economics. His role was to keep a watching brief on the product and engineering activities for Hennessy.

It was in 1953, too, that Hennessy made one of his most crucial decisions. Increasingly aware that in the new post-war world it was foolish for a major car producing company like Ford to rely on an outside contractor – Briggs – for all its bodies, since 1951 Hennessy had been trying to buy the British arm of Briggs Motor Bodies, which though a 62 per cent owned subsidiary of the Detroit company, also had British shareholders.

Although in the beginning Briggs had devoted itself to Ford alone, it had gradually widened its client list and by 1939 had a workforce of almost 3,000 and was devoting some 20 per cent of its activities to providing components and even

Using pretty girls in party frocks to demonstrate the rear legroom of the 1955 Anglia diverts the attention from the fact that the passenger seat is tipped right forward to maximise the effect of spaciousness.

An early Consul Convertible: built by Carbodies of Coventry, the convertible was previewed in Zephyr form at the 1951 Motor Show, but poor structural rigidity meant that production did not get fully under way until 1953 when an underfloor 'X'-shaped bracing member had been developed.

The Coronation Year Motor Show saw the fully-developed Zephyr Convertible with electro-hydraulically operated hood in pride of place on the Carbodies stand at Earls Court. Alongside is the Consul Convertible with manual hood. The more expensive Zephyr Convertible was more popular, with 4,048 produced against 3,749 Consuls.

complete bodies for some of Ford's rivals. The original Briggs factory had been designed to produce 60 bodies daily, but by the outbreak of war this had risen to over 180 a day. To alleviate some of the congestion caused by all this extra work, in 1938 Briggs bought the Dagenham River Plant 'a group of scattered and very inadequate buildings' on an 11-acre site outside the Ford estate. These buildings, said a post-war report, 'have been utilised to the maximum possible extent, but have never lent themselves to production on the Briggs pattern'.

During World War Two, Briggs expanded its activities to meet demand for aircraft components, developing seven extra factories on behalf of various government ministries, including a plant in Dundee where it made jerrycans. At its wartime peak, Briggs employed 23,000 workers, though this had dropped to less than 6,000 by 1948. Its factory at Southampton was part of the old Supermarine works where the prototype Spitfire had made its maiden flight and it also had a major works in Doncaster, along with a number of other locations including Croydon Airport. Another plant on a 2.5-acre site at Romford in Essex was acquired in the late 1940s.

Among Briggs's post-war clients were Austin, Rootes, Standard, Leyland and Chrysler – all Ford competitors – and the Yorkshire firm of Jowett, whose Javelin saloon, taking its styling cues from the pre-war Lincoln Zephyr, had created something of a sensation on the British market. But Briggs and Jowett had finally called it a day in December 1952 after Jowett had over-reached itself by trying to

make its own transmissions, which had proved unreliable. As it had struggled to fix the problems, bodies from Briggs were stockpiled around the little Yorkshire town of Idle where Jowett had been established since 1909, mounting up as fast as the piles of unpaid Briggs bills.

Briggs also had valuable aircraft industry contracts making engine cowlings for the Rolls-Royce Merlins installed in Tudor, York, Lancastrian and Lincoln aircraft and the de Havilland Mosquito, and for the radial installations in the Hawker Tempest and Sea Fury.

Things suddenly came to a head in 1953 with the death of company founder Walter O. Briggs and the threat that Chrysler, which was the biggest customer of the Detroit Briggs factories, would buy the American company and gain control of the Dagenham Briggs plant, too. Hennessy immediately rang Detroit and got an option from Briggs to purchase the company's British holdings valid for several weeks. Henry Ford II willingly approved 'Uncle Pat's' deal. Even though there was a strict government interdiction on the export of foreign currency, Hennessy boldly undertook to pay in dollars 'in the belief that there was some way of doing this'.

And indeed there was: his excellent links with the Treasury meant that approval for the expenditure of the dollars followed quickly.

Having paid £3.2 million for Briggs family and company shares, Ford then acquired the remaining privately-held shares by exchanging two Ford Motor Company ordinary shares and five shillings (£0.25) for each Briggs share, bringing the total cost of the Briggs purchase to £5.6 million.

Production of the Mk II Zephyr and Zodiac began at Dagenham on 19 January 1956, followed three weeks later by the Consul. Unlike their predecessors, the 'Three Graces' had been entirely styled in the Briggs studio in Dagenham.

End of an era: the last 103E Popular leaves the 'Y' line at Dagenham on 8 August 1953 as production is transferred to the Briggs plant in Doncaster, ending Thames-side manufacture of the small Ford range after 21 years.

The 'Low Line' version of the Mk II range went into production at the beginning of 1959. A new roof pressing reduced the height of the cars by some 1.5 inches, while a choice of 'new, spring-gay colours enhanced that "fine-car" finish'.

By any standards it was a bargain: and the possession of the Briggs Main and River Plants opened the way for further Ford expansion on the Dagenham site. Production had already trebled since the war, and in 1955 the plant would achieve its millionth post-war export, with the second millionth following five years later.

For Sir Patrick Hennessy, the Briggs takeover had also meant that a proper styling department could be established at Dagenham – and 'style' was the operative word. Like his great friend Sir William Lyons of Jaguar, Hennessy had an intuitive sense of style, and his influence on the shape of the Fords of the 1950s was crucial. Dr Tom Karen, who ultimately became head of Ogle Design, started his career at Briggs, and recalled that 'Sir Patrick was a great guy for design. He used to like to sit in the studio and chat to the designers.' However, John Frayling remembered that the stylists always used to put a deliberate mistake in their models so that Sir Patrick could find and correct it and feel that he had made a contribution.

The styling studio in what was still referred to as 'Briggs' had the air of a gentleman's club, with a part-time butler named George Makepeace Casey in yellow-and-black striped waistcoat, and in those

Safety was beginning to be a consideration in 1959, when the restyled fascia of the Mk II range included 'a cowl formed in shock-absorbent material'. This is the Consul, with a hub-centre horn push. Zephyr and Zodiac had a half-ring to operate the horn.

days senior styling artists wore bow ties. This may well have been the influence of Eric Archer, who had come from Rootes, and instituted what were known as 'sartorial days', when the stylists used to dress in their Sunday best.

But the profession of car stylist was a comparatively new one, and the roads into the studio were many and varied.

Dagenham's stylists were encouraged to indulge in flights of fancy to stimulate their imagination: this is a mid-1950s proposal for a Ford sports car.

One senior stylist, a dapper chap named Non Crook who sported a Vandyke beard and produced the most brilliant airbrush renderings, was described by company publicity as having been 'active in show business'. That was, in the broadest sense, true: but in Non's case, 'show business' meant that he had formerly painted giant portraits of film stars like Rita Hayworth across West End cinema facades.

Like the parent company in America, the Dagenham studio based its 'package' on the dimensions of a fictitious gentleman named 'Oscar', a mannequin based on the body measurements of 68,000 American troops 'to make him the nearest thing to the average man yet devised. If Oscar is comfortable, then the vast majority of other people will be too'.

Freed from the restrictions and shortages of the post-war austerity years, design was bursting forth in a riot of colours and shapes, as a Ford publicity leaflet

The Beachwagon was an unrealised 1950s concept for a seaside people-carrier by Briggs artist Charles J. Thompson using the 400E Thames 10/12cwt van introduced in 1957 as a basis.

Another mid-1950s proposal for a Ford sports car, this one produced by Charles Thompson, who joined Briggs Motor Bodies as an engineering draughtsman in 1949.

enthused: 'Soon Ford's Styling Studios may be working on turbo-cars: cars with smaller engines so that completely new shapes and designs can be introduced; cars with pressurised cabins to hurtle along the spaceways of the future at fantastic speeds... The ideas begin from many different sources: the jet planes that streak across the sky, the shapes and colours of fish, sometimes even the space fiction that people read. And basically they tend toward greater comfort, increased safety and jet age shapes.'

The stylists were encouraged to indulge their wildest design fancies, and their drawing boards glowed with surreal designs for rocket cars that 'may never go into production but could provide ideas for future designs or inspiration for headlamps, bonnet and roof lines or instrument panels... Long range thinking and planning is an important factor in car design and features normal today would have been thought fantastic 50 years ago.'

If the styling studio was a high point of the Briggs acquisition, a definite low was the erratic labour relations climate caused by a workforce which hadn't come to terms with the Ford takeover. Peter Kennedy, who had just joined the Briggs styling studio as a trainee, remembered the sight of a Briggs walk-out with awe: 'The strikers poured out of the building like water – it was terrifying in its scale.'

A prime source of irritation was a union official known as the 'Bellringer', who insisted on his right to call union meetings during working hours by ringing a handbell. Matters came to a head during a shopfloor walkout when Briggs's general manager Allen Barke – who had joined Ford during 1932 in the very earliest days of the Dagenham plant and run Leamington Foundry after the war – refused to take the ringleaders of the strike back after the dispute was settled. He stood his ground in the face of threatened militancy. Labour relations at Briggs improved markedly after that.

An appointment which was to have great consequences for Ford-Britain came in 1954, when Terry Beckett was appointed styling manager at Briggs. Beckett – who was promoted to manager of the new product planning division in 1955 after its first manager, Martin Tustin, left to join Standard – was to help shape the models that gave Ford market dominance in the 1960s.

This swoopy clay created at the end of 1957 was the first design proposal for the Mk III Zephyr/Zodiac line. It was erased and followed by a couple of concepts by American senior stylist Engel, which were rejected as 'too American'.

Forty years on, Beckett – now Sir Terence – remembered how stimulating he found his new job: 'It was very exciting to see these designs for weeks and to go into the street and think this is all very dull – for we had been looking into the future.' Importantly, Beckett instituted a three-pronged approach, with separate departments planning small, medium and large cars.

Dagenham's studio – familiarly known as 'the Odeon' – became a sought-after centre of design skills: Colin Chapman, looking for styling talent to help him at his infant Lotus company, recruited three gifted designers from Ford, who initially moonlighted at Chapman's little Hornsey works while working days at Dagenham. They were John Frayling, a skilled clay modeller from New Zealand, who translated accountant Peter Kirwan-Taylor's design for the Lotus Elite into a three-dimensional model, using special heat-setting clay that had to be imported from Ford's styling department in Dearborn, interior designer Peter Cambridge and South African Ron Hickman, who had worked as a clay modeller under Colin Neale before training as a designer. Famed for his invention of that brilliant DIY aid, the Workmate, Hickman was design director at Lotus from 1958–67. Then there was Tom Karen, an adept sketcher of futuristic concept cars, whose post-Ford portfolio at Ogle Design included the Daimler SX250 prototype, the Reliant Scimitar and Robin and the futuristic Bond Bug three-wheeler.

This is 'Breakaway', Colin Neale's 1958 suggestion for the Mk III range. It never got past the full-size mock-up stage, though its use of a reverse-rake 'C' pillar and space-age styling features were adventurous, reflecting 1950s confidence in a 'Dan Dare' future.

Once the dreaming was over, designs chosen to go forward for production were modelled full-size in clay over a wooden armature by a team led by 'Little' George Saunders. This clay served as reference for the hand-beaten panels that made up the first prototypes, which were reviewed 'in a garden not even big enough for a game of tennis. The flower beds guarding the lawn in a thin line of colour are flanked on two sides by a white-washed wall and on the other two by the fluted glass windows of the studios where over 30 specialists work. It is in this garden that colour combinations and interior fabrics are often considered in natural lighting.'

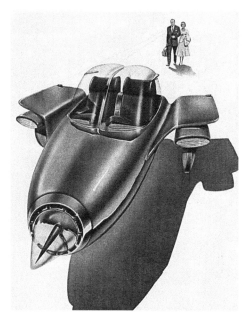

Typical of the 'fanciful scheming on paper' that emanated from the Briggs styling studio, this jet-propelled dream car was claimed to 'bridge the gap between the impractical stylist's doodle and the practical models of the assembly line'.

Although Ford's British styling studios were to move on twice from Dagenham in the 1960s, and though in their new locations the daylight review areas were no more than prosaic concrete-paved courtyards, Ford employees still refer to them as 'the garden' in memory of that little patch of greensward at Dagenham.

Around the time of the Briggs takeover, the studios began working on the successors to the Consul and Zephyr range. These 'Mk II' models were slightly larger than their predecessors and the engines were increased in capacity to cope by increasing both bore and stroke to give swept volumes of 1.7 and 2.6 litres for four and six-cylinder versions respectively.

Again, the Consul, Zephyr and Zodiac designations were used, though the Zodiac was now a stand-alone version with gold-plated badges, a special grille, two-tone paint, a heater as standard and an elaborate 'washboard panel finished in gold' across its rear end, adding a couple of inches to the overall length.

Intriguingly, the grille design for the Zephyr was strongly influenced by the contemporary Aston Martin DB3: 'It was certainly discussed,' recalled Ron Hickman.

A British-market 'first' for the new model was a combined ignition-starter key, a feature which has since become universal. Another feature new to a British family car was an interior light that came on automatically when the door was opened.

The first hand-built prototype, a black Zephyr Six, edged out of the Rainham Engineering Department on a dark December night in 1954 and drove round the car park 'watched by an excited crowd of engineering, design and styling experts'. In mid-January 1955 the second and third prototypes – a Zodiac and a Consul – left Dagenham by road for 'a secret destination in Europe – a little-known mountain area in Germany where the only spectators were the inhabitants of a few scattered villages and stately pine forests' – accompanied by a Mk I Zephyr for comparison.

The wintry weather, carolled Ford, helped security: 'For the Ford men the snow's white cloak wrapped the expedition with an air of almost dedication, and an enemy to most drivers was an ally in safeguarding the secrets of the prototypes'.

Based in a chalet hidden in the pine forest, the test programme went on for several months, joined by prototype number five, a Zephyr. Apart from road testing over 'cross-country tracks... badly made-up highways, long stretches of shattering pavé and miles of high-speed motoring on the famous German autobahns', cars were left out overnight in the open in 40 degrees of frost to test cold starting.

Suspension testing was carried out on the tough colonial roads of Kenya, despite the threat of Mau Mau terrorism, and further endurance testing took place on 'Ford's own proving ground', with its high speed circuit, stretches of corrugated road and pavé; a water splash and Dagenham's 'dust tunnel' were also used in testing the new models in 'one of the most intense proving programmes in automobile history'.

Though the Mk II convertibles – again modified by Carbodies – represented less than 2.5 per cent of total production, they were included in the range because Sir Patrick Hennessy, newly-appointed chairman of Ford-Britain, liked them. He kept his Mk II Zodiac convertible long into his retirement.

Promoted as the 'Three Graces', the new models sold well, with Abbott 'Farnham' estates, automatic transmission and a Zodiac convertible with power hood being added to the range at the 1956 Earls Court Motor Show. A reflection on changing production costs was that a new 'nylonweave' upholstery material was available as an option at the same price as leather trim!

In 1954 Sir Patrick Hennessy had announced an ambitious programme of modernisation and expansion, to be financed entirely out of retained earnings, which would almost double factory floor space and enable some 2,000 vehicles to be built a day.

Central to the programme was the remodelling and re-equipping of the Briggs facilities and the construction at a cost of £10 million of a 250,000sq ft new paint, trim and assembly (PTA) building on the 48-acre Ford sports ground at Dagenham. This was on the opposite side of Kent Avenue – the main approach to the Ford plant – to Briggs. The new PTA building would be linked to the older building by a continuously-moving overhead conveyor enclosed in a 725 foot-long bridge. This was to carry the unpainted bodyshells of all Ford's car lines and would be air-conditioned to prevent any rusting of the bare metal.

The new building was designed to handle up to a thousand bodies and powertrains for six different models at a time and would contain nine miles of conveyor track controlled by 1,200 miles of electric wiring. Totally automated, the new system contained the facility to move bodies from one production line to another yet still complete them on schedule.

The addition of the PTA building increased Dagenham output capacity dramatically: in 1934 the plant had built just 57,195 vehicles, while in 1959 it built 472,857.

While it had taken 15 years to build Dagenham's millionth vehicle, the second million was achieved in just 10, leaving the line during 1956.

To solve some of Dagenham's space problems before the new plant came on-stream, in August 1955 production of the hair-shirt basic 103E Popular – 'the world's cheapest car' – had been transferred from the old 'Y' line that had been rolling at Dagenham since 1932 to the Briggs plant at Doncaster. A glimpse of the less demanding standards of the 1950s motorist is shown by the fact that in 1953–4, more 103E Populars left Dagenham (66,933) than the combined total of the new 100E Anglias and Prefects (60,511).

Similarly, the parts distribution system, which had hitherto grown haphazardly, was to be concentrated in a building 'as big as five football pitches' on a 15-acre site that Ford had bought on the new Belhus estate between South Ockendon and Aveley, a few miles east of Dagenham. Opened in 1957, in 1958 it became home to 'Leo', the British motor industry's first in-house computer, a massive assembly of thousands of valves and miles of wiring that prepared the parts ordering paperwork from a huge stack of punched cards.

With a workforce equivalent to the population of a small town, Dagenham placed considerable demands on the local transport infrastructure: London Transport actually had its own on-site office where two inspectors coordinated the flow of buses taking workers to and from the factory.

These 1957 Consuls both carry licence plates that indicate they are registered under the 'Home Delivery Export Scheme', in which overseas visitors could take delivery of a new Ford, use it on holiday in Britain, then export it free of UK tax.

In the 1950s, Ford estate cars, which then represented a relatively small percentage of production, were converted by coachbuilders Abbott of Farnham, who removed the boot lid and rear window of the saloon body, extended the roof and fitted rear side panels and tailgate. This is a 1959 Low-Line Consul Estate.

While the 'Mk II' range was still on the drawing board, Terry Beckett had sent a Briggs designer named Colin MacGregor to work in the new Birmingham research centre on a replacement for the obsolescent 'sit up and beg' 103E Popular. The newly-recruited engineering staff had done some preliminary design work, but, said MacGregor, the scale model that they showed him 'looked like a jazzed-up A30 – it really was a mess!'

So he started again, and, in the interests of production cost-saving, designed a car with a thin sheet-metal roof spot-welded to the body side pressings. The same financial restraints also compelled the use of a flat rear window, and the only solution to this problem was to use a daring reverse-rake rear window, which had the added bonuses that it gave a generous boot lid opening and kept clean in rain or snow. The idea had been suggested by Sir Patrick Hennessy after he had seen a Pininfarina-bodied Fiat 600 at the March 1955 Geneva Show. That two-door four-seater, built in just 15 days, gained extra headroom in the rear seats and a wider engine compartment lid by the pioneering use of a a reverse-rake rear window. 'The Fiat window was only about six inches deep,' recalled

The 8–10 seat 'Estate Car' was a standard body option on the 400E Thames van which became popular with musicians: it featured in a Ford publicity film *Bandwagon*, featuring the Cy Laurie jazz band.

Launched in March 1957, the forward-control 500E Thames Trader truck range was produced in capacities of up to 7 tons. Lincoln Cars, on London's Great West Road, housed Ford's import-export division as well as the motor sport department. The building had been occupied in the early 1930s by the French Delage company.

The 1957 Thames Trader was a highly versatile chassis: this short wheelbase example is fitted with a high-lift tower conversion.

former senior stylist Colin Neale. 'You needed to get the proportions right on a larger car.' Admittedly, before the Anglia, the same styling feature had been copied on the 1958 Lincoln Continental designed in the Special Projects studio of Ford-US senior stylist Elwood Engel, who was a regular visitor to Dagenham, but it gave the new small car a distinctively perky look.

MacGregor's prototype was ready in 1955. It was 'very spartan inside', with a single 'pod' instrument panel containing just a speedometer and fuel gauge, no heater and 'hammock' type canvas seats on tubular frames. Vacuum-formed inner door panels were a bold step and there was even talk of making the body out of glass fibre. An idea years ahead of its time was the proposal for a pickup version with a detachable van top.

Bizarrely, MacGregor chose a colour scheme of lilac body with purple interior trim for the prototype, for which an experimental two-stroke power unit was built with help from Skoda and DKW engineers, but this proved a 'terrible, noisy engine'.

Back at the Dagenham studio, work was going on to design a replacement for the 100E, and they picked up on

Production of the 105E Anglia began at Dagenham in September 1959, but was transferred to the company's new factory at Halewood on Merseyside in March 1963.

In the new Paint, Trim and Assembly plant opened at the end of 1959, bodies went through a comprehensive rust-proofing and priming process before being given their final coat of low-bake enamel. This Anglia body is ready to move on to the trim shop.

some of the features of the Birmingham 'New Popular', such as the reverse rake screen for this 'Sunbird' project. It then became apparent that the Birmingham project would be ready for market before the Dagenham design, so the 100E replacement was redesignated the 'Consul Classic' and the Birmingham project was uprated and re-engineered under Fred Hart's supervision to become the 105E Anglia. The cost-cutting features were shelved and the bonnet design was altered.

A new short-stroke 997cc overhead valve engine was developed under Dagenham's chief engine engineer, Allan Worters, and codenamed 'Kent' (because that was where he lived) and the new car was the first from Ford-Britain to have a four-speed gearbox (though the company's commercial vehicles could be had with four-speed boxes before the war).

One proposal which failed to make it past the scale model stage was a sports version of the 105E designed as an 'unauthorised project' by Ron Hickman as a riposte to the forthcoming Austin-Healey Sprite, which had been spotted on test by keen-eyed Ford delivery truck drivers at the secret track of the Motor Industry

Blacklisted in America, film producer Joseph Losey worked in Britain during the 1950s, where he directed a light-hearted film entitled *First on the Road* for the Ford Film Unit to promote the new 105E Anglia, in between producing serious feature films like *Chance Meeting* and *The Concrete Jungle*.

Research Association in Warwickshire and sketched by Ford stylist Eric Archer from their descriptions. Hickman incoporated many original ideas in his 105E sports project, including glass-fibre bumpers and what he believes was the first lift-off plastic 'Targa top'. This was inspired by the uncertain labour relations of the Briggs plant: 'Ford was constantly being held up by industrial action in the trim shop,' he recalls, 'so instead of using a sewn hood, I incorporated a lift-off roof panel. For the same reason I also used slush-moulded slabs for the seats instead of the sewn seats.'

The Anglia was launched in the autumn of 1959, though its claim to be the 'the world's most exciting light car' was rather mitigated by the almost simultaneous appearance of the new BMC Mini – but the Anglia was the only one of the two to bring its makers profits.

The British Motor Corporation had none of the product planning disciplines of Dagenham, and though they had costed the Mini against a comparable Ford product, they had used the soon-to-be-replaced 100E Anglia as their benchmark. When Ford bought an early Mini for Terry Beckett's product planning department to dismantle and cost analyse they found that their rivals could not possibly be making a profit at the price they were asking.

At a dealer meeting held on the Crystal Palace race track to launch the 105E Anglia in 1959, Ford also showed a variety of commercials, like this 400E Thames with a tower wagon conversion by Eagle of Warwick.

Dagenham's joint managing director Allen Barke called on BMC managing director George Harriman at his London office for an off-the-record meeting: 'Look here, George,' he said, 'We've costed your new Mini and you can't possibly be making any money on it. If you raise your price so you're making a profit, we'll raise the price of the Anglia by the same amount.'

But Harriman was adamant: 'The product will push the price,' was his gnomic response. Loosely translated, this signified: 'Sell enough cars and the profits will take care of themselves.'

History was to prove him sadly wrong: it would be decades before BMC and its successors made a penny profit on the Mini, although they built millions of them.

Chapter Eight

MARKET FORCES

W HILE Dearborn had established its Ford-International division in 1949 to coordinate the activities of its overseas subsidiaries, in reality a decade later the European companies still continued as 'more or less private domains of the local management'.

However, Dearborn was moving toward closer control of those 'private domains'. Toward the end of 1959, plans began to be put in place to acquire all the remaining privately-owned shares of Ford-Britain. The plan was to enable Ford of America to increase its operational flexibility, to improve the coordination of its European and

The giant Ford logo on the power house was a feature of the Dagenham waterfront for four decades, but eventually had to be taken down when its fixings became unsafe.

The main assembly building in the early 1960s. The main factory gate is where the roads converge to the right of the island car park.

American manufacturing facilities and to further integrate its worldwide product lines and operations.

On 14 November the following year, Dearborn announced that it was to bid $20.50 (£7.25) for each £1 ordinary share, amounting to an estimated total of £128.5 million.

Henry Ford II commented: 'In recent years, competition in world automotive markets has become broader and more intense. The development of the Common Market and the European Free Trade Area in the years ahead is likely to accelerate this trend. In these circumstances, we believe that it is important for us, as a world manufacturer, to pursue this objective if we are to be able to compete effectively.

'One of our major objectives is to be able to achieve greater operational efficiency and greater marketing effectiveness in both countries. If we are successful in attaining this objective, we shall have a product position and a cost position which should enable us to compete more effectively throughout the world.

'As far as we are concerned, we intend that Ford Motor Company Limited's

Managing director Allen Barke with Princess Margaret at the Motor Show. Ford has long held a Royal Warrant: one of its more unusual orders was in the 1980s for a Granada stretched 18 inches to accommodate the Queen Mother's Corgis.

The archetypal Ford of the 1960s was the Cortina. Amazingly, its chief stylist Roy Brown had previously been responsible for designing the Lincoln Futura – a concept car that became TV's kitsch *Batmobile* – and the disastrous Edsel.

In a lingering echo of the 'Woodie' estate cars that had been one of Dagenham's popular niche models in the 1930s and 1940s, the 1963 Cortina Super Estate 1500 boasted 'Di-Noc' faux wood panelling on its flanks and tailgate.

operations shall continue under the able direction of Sir Patrick Hennessy without change in its employment policy or in its development programme.'

Even though the presidency of Dwight D. Eisenhower was drawing to an end, the news of the proposed takeover alarmed the outgoing administration in Washington. At the beginning of December 1960, after a series of leaks and denials, the Treasury Department finally confirmed that it had asked Ford to consider the impact of its bid on America's deteriorating balance of payments.

Despite its cleverly-designed monocoque bodyshell, the Cortina still called for hand-finishing of its seams on the Dagenham production line.

Henry Ford II's response was adamant: 'In telephone conversations with Secretary Anderson in mid-November the projected transaction between the Ford Motor Company (United States) and the minority shareholders of Ford, England, was discussed. Suggestions made by Mr Anderson at that time have been given every consideration. But at no time then, or since, has it been requested by Mr Anderson or by any other government official that we withdraw our offer.'

Indeed, stressed *The Daily Telegraph*, Anderson could not legally have made such a request: 'All he can do is to draw the company's attention pointedly to the balance of payments position and leave the decision to them.'

Carry on camping: this pre-production publicity shot of the 1963 De Luxe *(left)* and Super 1500 Cortina Estates reveals the exterior trim differences between the two models.

Sir Patrick Hennessy confirmed that his board had found the preliminary documents satisfactory from Ford-Britain's point of view and was going ahead with the American offer.

Henry Ford II pointed out that the purchase would mean that Ford-US would have a far larger stake in the British

company than in all other operations outside the United States combined: 'I think it should be agreed that we would have added incentive to promote the interests, the well-being and the prosperity of Ford of England in every way practicable, as we have always done in the past and intend to continue to do so in the future.'

The offer documents were duly sent out in mid-December, with Ford's offer remaining at $20.50, with the deadline for acceptance set for 3pm on 10 January 1961. Additionally, shareholders would still receive the second interim dividend due on 7 January. The Treasury approved the deal on condition that the offer was made in sterling rather than dollars to meet British exchange control regulations.

'In the face of a declining trend in the second half of 1960 which is proving to be more severe than was foreseen', said *The Times*, '...this is no situation for a

Ford's European marketing policy saw the 400E Thames van, seen here in Holland, competing with the German Taunus Transit in many continental markets: they called it the 'two fishing lines' policy.

In the early 1960s, all Ford commercial vehicle production left the increasingly congested Dagenham factory: this view of KLM's Heathrow fleet dates from 1963, when production of the Anglia van *(left)* transferred to the new Halewood plant and the Thames van and truck range was built at Langley in Buckinghamshire.

Many thousands of Cortinas were shipped out of Dagenham for export markets: surprisingly, they still had to be craned aboard the freighters. The day of the roll on-roll off freighter was still some way in the future.

competitive bidder... the general impression in the City is that a large proportion of shareholders will now accept.'

Nevertheless, it came as a rude shock, recalled Ford-Britain's joint managing director Allen Barke, that when he attended a Ford convention in January 1961 Ernie Breech, the retiring chairman of the Ford Motor Company, stood up and announced that Ford-America had bought all the outstanding shares in Ford-Britain. Barke had to take an embarrassed bow.

On 23 January, Lord Hampden, the managing director of Lazard Brothers, merchant bankers to Ford-US, handed a cheque for £119,595,645 12s to Frank Keighley of the National Provincial Bank for the credit of Ford-Britain. At the time, it was the biggest cheque ever negotiated.

The role of Dagenham as a self-sufficient manufacturing site began to change radically in a general diaspora of the managerial functions during the 1960s. First of the key divisions to go were styling, engineering and prototype work, which moved into a new extension built on the north end of the Aveley Parts depot in August 1960.

It was there that a young product planner named Alex Trotman, who had joined Ford at Dagenham as a student in 1955, where he spent three years as a progress

Cortinas awaiting shipment by train from Dagenham, served by its own branch line coming right into the heart of the plant.

chaser, ferrying urgently needed parts to the production line in the back of his ancient Austin Seven to keep production flowing, began the steady climb through Ford's management ranks that ultimately led him to the chairmanship of the parent Ford Motor Company in Dearborn, the first British-born holder of that high office.

Dagenham workers buff down the bonnet of a part-finished Mk 1 Cortina bodyshell with wet sanders in the Paint, Trim and Assembly building.

It's easy to see why Ford had to decentralise: in 1961, the year in which the Langley heavy vehicle line went on-stream following a £70 million investment, Dagenham built almost 416,000 cars, vans, trucks and tractors and almost 489,000 engines. Even with the new PTA building, the 30-year-old factory was just running out of space. Crucially, plans were approved for a new £13 million administration building on the site of the Essex Regiment's old barracks at Warley in Essex. No longer would Dagenham's river-front office building be the epicentre of Ford activities in Britain.

In 1962 Ford-International established an office in Brussels to of all the European Ford companies except Britain and Germany. Its head was a former sports coach named Leo Beebe. He had been second-in-command to Ensign Henry Ford in a

'Slipper-dipping' a Cortina bodyshell in the Dagenham PTA building followed rust-proofing and sealing: the bodies then proceeded to the spray booths for priming.

school for machinists' mates, pipefitters and technicians at the Rouge Plant during the war and joined the Ford Motor Company after it. As manager of public and governmental affairs, he organised a world marketing conference in Paris for around 500 Ford executives from all over the world, at the end of which he was appointed director of marketing for the Brussels office. His job was to devise ways of integrating Ford companies all over Europe.

Dagenham and Cologne were still going their own separate ways on products, but in contrast with Dagenham, Ford-Germany still needed help from Dearborn on major new model engineering. At the beginning of the 1960s, Cologne was working with Ford-US on a $35 million programme to develop a new family car which was to be marketed on both sides of the Atlantic. Codenamed 'Cardinal' after the little red North American bird, this model broke new ground for Ford, for it was front-wheel driven. The scheme was for all the engine/powertrain units to be built in Cologne, with 1.5-litre versions shipped to the US to be installed in bodyshells built in Ford's Louisville plant, while a 1.2-litre 'Cardinal' would be sold in Europe.

Early in 1960, on one of his regular trips to Dearborn, Sir Patrick Hennessy saw the prototype Cardinal and at once the old Anglo-German rivalries flared up. The carefully-laid new model programme was thrown to the wind and the forthcoming 'Consul Classic' suddenly became a stopgap as Sir Patrick Hennessy returned home determined to develop a British rival to the new model to outflank the Germans. Production plans were altered and body pressings for the Classic – and a special 2+2 coupé 'Capri' version developed as a 'personal car' as a sort of British equivalent of the American Ford Thunderbird to please Sir Patrick – were produced on short-life 'Kirksite' dies rather than the steel dies used for long production runs.

Designer Roy Haynes, who left Ford to join British Leyland in 1966, recalled: 'The Capri could have had proper back seats if Ford had been willing to re-tool the boot lid so that it didn't take up as much space – but they weren't.'

Although at the beginning of 1961 Lee Iacocca, Dearborn's newly-appointed vice-president of the Ford Division, thought the Cardinal had 'lousy styling… a loser' and immediately killed off the American end of the deal – a pet project of his 'bean-counter' predecessor Robert McNamara, who had resigned to join the newly-elected John F. Kennedy's cabinet as Secretary of Defense – the car was still due to be introduced in Germany under Cologne's popular Taunus brand in the autumn of 1962.

Hennessy realised that trying to follow the technically-advanced front-wheel-drive German/US design would take too long, and ordered his engineers to develop a superior car following the proven rear-drive layout. Tongue-in-cheek, his staff named their project 'Archbishop' to outrank the Cardinal. To increase its family appeal, they developed a car that fell between the popular 'C' and 'D' size classes.

To do this, the new model needed a bodyshell that was

'Styled at Dagenham by Dagenham people', the Classic – or, to give it its full name, Consul Classic 315 –had the raked-back 'C' pillar that Sir Patrick Hennessy had first seen on a Pininfarina Fiat 600 concept car at the March 1955 Geneva Show.

Britain's Thunderbird: the 1962 Capri was Sir Patrick Hennessy's personal project and had a non-standard production code 'SB60' – presumably for 'Special Build'. The 'floating' star motifs in the grille of the Capri and Classic that recalled Ford's 'Five Stars Ahead' slogan were the brainchild of stylist Ron Hickman.

cheap to produce, yet light and strong. The prime mover in this development was Ford chief body engineer Don Ward, who saw the task as 'eliminating the unwanted passenger'. This meant saving about 150lb compared with a conventional monocoque. Ward took the bold step of recruiting stressman Dennis Roberts, who had joined Briggs in 1957 from Bristol Aircraft, to establish a structures department at Dagenham. Roberts was uniquely qualified: before working for Bristol, he had graduated from the Ford Scholarship scheme which had been set up in 1937 to train future senior engineers.

It was an inspired choice: using techniques normally used to design aeroplane fuselages, Roberts established a test shop where bodies could be subjected to scientific torsion and bending tests. 'From what I'd learned in the aircraft industry about the testing of aircraft fuselages and wings, I thought I had perhaps a better idea of how big integral structures behave.'

Although Ford was already using computers, Roberts carried out his complex calculations on paper with dramatic results. 'I recognised that there were certain bits of structure which contributed very little to the overall stiffness, and wherever that occurred, we took them out. Progressively we got the bodyshell down to something like 630lb for the body-in-white, against nearly 800lb for the Classic.' The unwanted passenger had been eliminated.

So despite the theoretical weight advantages of front-wheel drive, the apparently orthodox Archbishop weighed almost the same as the slightly smaller Taunus; it was also a little faster and a little more fuel-efficient.

Sir Patrick Hennessy played a major role in the development of the new car; it was

If you can't solve a problem, hold an inquiry. In 1965, when the British motor industry lost six million days through strike action, Jack Scamp was appointed by Labour Prime Minister Harold Wilson to head a new Motor Industry Joint Council to investigate the problem. Here is Scamp *(centre)* inspecting Dagenham's body plant, 'a persistent battleground' and the focus of Ford union trouble.

after all his baby. Maybe his boldness here cost him his next pet project, a small but roomy front-wheel drive minicar, which was kicked into touch by the Ford 'beancounters' and never passed the prototype stage.

Heading the styling team in the new Aveley studio was a Canadian ex-dance band crooner named Roy Brown, who had studied industrial design at the Detroit Art Academy and worked on 'everything from helicopters to pencil sharpeners... radios, motor cruisers, coloured glass products, Cadillacs and Oldsmobiles' before joining Ford in 1953. His initial assignment in the Dearborn studios was the design of the Lincoln Futura concept car, which ultimately became the TV 'Batmobile'.

Brown was, in a sense, 'in the wilderness', for he had previously headed the team that had styled the disastrous Edsel, which had just recorded a monumental loss of some $350 million for Ford-US. His first task on arriving in England had been to head up the design team for the replacement for the Mk II Consul/Zephyr range, initial studies for which had been carried out by the Mk II's designer Colin Neale before he was posted to Dearborn.

Ideas by Neale and visiting American stylist Elwood Engel were rejected as 'too American', though after Neale had moved to Dearborn, Sir Patrick wrote him a frank letter: 'We are still in trouble with our Mark III. For one thing it seems difficult to marry the Galaxie type of roof to the design below the belt line. We have tried a number of variants, yet are not happy.'

So Ford sought outside help from Frua of Turin. But the Frua design, too, was found wanting – 'though it did act as a catalyst, goading the Dagenham studio into

Dagenham was an export powerhouse in the 1960s: in 1963, for instance, it actually exported more cars than it sold at home, shipping 229,569 cars overseas against 225,134 domestic products.

action,' recalled Peter Kennedy – and the final form of the 1962 Mk III range took shape under Brown's leadership, with many of the more distinctive features being sketched out by Briggs-trained Charles Thompson. Incidentally, the Mk III received regular prime-time TV coverage as the 'star' vehicle in the popular BBC TV police series *Z Cars*, while the Mk III Zodiac was the first 100mph car produced at Dagenham.

Of the various styling themes proposed by Brown's team for the new 'Archbishop', the preferred design had a pronounced tapered flute along the bodysides, terminating in vestigial fins. The mock-up had neat, arrow-shaped rear light indicators incorporated in the rear fins, but Hennessy preferred a circular lamp unit

divided into three 120-degree segments. It looked like the emblem of the Campaign for Nuclear Disarmament, and was nicknamed the 'Ban-the-Bomb' lamp.

When it came to choosing a name for the new car, Ford-Britain's product committee originally suggested the old 'Prefect' nomenclature. Then it decreed that the entire range

More than 10,000 people worked in Dagenham's Metal Stamping and Body Division in the 1960s. In the £6 million Press Shop, 170 giant presses, some weighing 400 tons and capable of exerting a pressure of 1,200 tons, worked non-stop, converting 600 tons of sheet metal into 1,800 car bodies every working day.

Shipping Mk 1 Cortinas and Mk III Zephyrs and Zodiacs out of Dagenham aboard specially-built 'Cartic' rail transporter wagons.

After Sir Patrick Hennessy, seen here showing a family group round Dagenham, retired as chairman of Ford-Britain in 1968 when he reached 70, his links with the Ford family ensured that he was retained as a consultant until his death in 1981.

should carry the 'Consul' name, which Hennessy for some reason felt should be carried by all the larger British models. When the first press photos were taken, the prototypes were badged 'Consul 215' and 'Consul 225'.

Next, Sir Patrick, inspired by the Consul Capri, suggested that the Archbishop be called the 'Caprino,' but was dissuaded when he learned that this was Italian for 'goat dung.' But it was the venue of the 1960 Winter Olympics that at the 11th hour gave the Archbishop the name by which it would enter motoring history: 'Cortina'. Fortunately, no one picked up the Italian dictionary that time, for in addition to being a fashionable ski resort in the Dolomites, Cortina is also Italian for 'curtains'.

Launched as the 'Consul Cortina' in September 1962, the new car was an instant success. Its power unit was an 1198cc derivative of the 997cc oversquare engine designed for the Anglia. Priced at £639, between the Anglia and Consul Classic, the Cortina exemplified Ford's concern about production costs and in fact would contribute some 50 percent of Ford-Britain's car line profits for years. By the spring of 1963, output had reached 1,200 units a day.

Like the Model Y 30 years earlier, the Cortina moved Ford-Britain into a new market sector and eventually gave the

When Dagenham stylists' ideas for the Mk III Zephyr/Zodiac line were rejected as 'too American', Italian designer Pietro Frua was called in to help. His design, too, was rejected, though some elements like the roofline, curved side windows and rear quarters were retained in the final version of the Zodiac.

An early Mk III Zephyr leaving Southend Airport aboard a Carvair freighter flying the Channel Air Bridge ferry service.

British company back the leadership of the British market that it had lost to Morris in the early 1920s.

The first chance that the rival designs had to go head-to-head was at a marketing conference held by Ford-International at Montlhéry, a banked racing circuit south of Paris, in the summer of 1962. Senior Ford executives from all over the world gathered to try the new Cortina and Taunus 12M siblings against each other. This was no relaxed product appraisal but an aggressive sales meeting at which Ford-Britain and Ford-Germany competed against one another to sell their new family cars to other Ford companies.

Zephyrs and Anglias converge on the Dagenham Jetty ready to be exported. In 1962, half Britain's car exports were Fords, worth £140 million. They were sold in 168 different foreign territories on five continents, 'in fact, almost everywhere there is a road or track for them to run on'.

Terry Beckett of the Dagenham Product Planning department had the task of 'selling' the Cortina to the assembled might of Ford-International: 'John Andrews (the head of Ford-Germany) was so convinced that we were in an inferior position – their car being front-wheel-drive and engineered in America and ours being rather traditional – that he said to me: "I'll give you the choice – do you want to present first or second?"

'I said: "Oh, first please, if I've got a choice."

'We went out to Montlhéry the next day. Each of us had 30-odd cars, their 12M and our Cortina, and they were having problems with carburation. Every one of their cars had to be withdrawn from the track during the trial – and ours steamed merrily on. They performed beautifully!

'I well remember asking Filmer Paradise, the Managing Director of Ford-Italiana, "Well, Fil, what do you make of it?" And he said: "Well, you've clearly shown today on this track that your car is a better performer. I'd add that it's better styled."

'So from being in that "perceived-to-be-inferior" slot, we really did come out as the winner!'

So it proved on the international market-place: by the time the original Cortina went out of production in 1966, a total of over 1 million had been sold. In the same period, Ford-Germany had sold 680,000 Taunus. Winners and losers – it was an odd game for two companies that were supposed to be part of the same organisation to play.

Like the Model Y, early Cortinas had an embarrassing transmission fault: some gearboxes, which were a new design using Porsche-type synchromesh for a snappy change, were assembled lacking a crucial oilway, which caused the box to seize without warning. This happened to the Cortina driven by the assistant editor of the trade magazine Motor Trader and he went off the road backwards at speed between two stanchions of a road sign. Such was the professionalism of Ford's press office in those days that when he rang Dagenham to complain a soft answer turned away his wrath and nothing of the incident appeared in print.

Ford's public relations had in fact suffered a sea-change, which arose from the very different personalities of Sir Patrick Hennessy and his Old Etonian public relations manager Maurice Buckmaster.

Jim Clark corners in his trademark Lotus-Cortina attitude: his skilled driving earned him the British Racing & Sports Car Club Championship title in 1964. The versatile Grand Prix ace even rallied the Lotus-Cortina with aplomb.

Colin Chapman's links with Ford came through Walter Hayes, who had employed him as a freelance motoring columnist in his Fleet Street days. The combination of Chapman and Jim Clark was a winning one, both for Ford and for Lotus.

The cottage-assembly methods used in the little Lotus factory at Cheshunt drove the Ford staff coordinating the Lotus-Cortina project to despair. 'Lotus don't even know what a bloody torque wrench is!' lamented a despairing Ford engineer.

Hennessy felt that Buckmaster was too grand, and that as a consequence, Ford's public image was flagging. In 1962, with the launch of the Cortina imminent, he asked his wartime colleague Lord Beaverbrook, proprietor of the *Daily Express*, to recommend a likely candidate for the job. Beaverbrook recommended 38-year-old Walter Hayes, who had recently resigned as associate editor of the *Daily Mail*. Hayes had previously been editor of the *Sunday Dispatch* and, although he was not a motoring man by background, had employed Lotus founder Colin Chapman on a freelance basis to contribute a 'new type of motoring column'.

Recalled Harry Calton, who had joined Ford as a teenager in the mid-1950s: 'Walter Hayes inherited a staff which enjoyed little respect within its own organisation. As a result our morale was extremely low. Within hours of arriving at Dagenham he informed us that as the editor of the *Sunday Dispatch* he had always instructed his journalists to bypass PR departments.

'However, through a number of extremely shrewd appointments from both inside and outside Ford, within a matter of months he had created a PR team that was the envy of the motor industry. It certainly commanded the respect of the Ford organisation.

'In those days, such was the Dagenham factory's size and scale that it was easy to ignore the outside world. Management traditionally wore blue suits allegedly supplied by a tailor working to a Ford specification and everyone recognised his place in the order of things.

The Dagenham-built Cortina GT of Peter Hughes and Billy Young won the 1964 East African Safari Rally, garnering an impressive bonnetful of trophies in the process. Cortinas won the manufacturers' team prize, too.

'The arrival of Walter Hayes heralded a wind of change. An inveterate pipe smoker, he dressed with a modern sense of style – courtesy of Savile Row – and when he was not prowling around the offices of his staff consulting and advising, he was seated at his typewriter writing press releases and strategy papers.

'The pipe was almost his undoing. Dagenham's highly varnished wooden waste paper bins were not made to receive pipe ash and inevitably he set fire to his office early one afternoon. While the Ford fire service saved the Dagenham office building from destruction, Walter busied himself with an impromptu meeting in the Press Office.

'His skill and flair brought dramatic results while raising many disapproving eyebrows at Ford. He was not prepared merely to communicate management decisions to the world outside Dagenham but insisted on being a member of all the major operating committees within the company.

'Journalists were encouraged to visit Ford and to drive Ford products for extended periods ahead of their public introduction. Through his influence on product committees, Walter persuaded Ford management to build performance derivatives of their cars.'

When the Cortina was launched, it was apparent that it was somewhat lacking in excitement. In 1962 Sir Patrick Hennessy had proposed a 'Saxon' two-seat coupé variant, but the prototype had been sent to Dearborn for appraisal and never heard of again. Hayes conceived another route: 'A performance version seemed one obvious way of adding excitement, because the heart of the Cortina was one of the greatest engines the world has ever known. I don't really think that's an exaggeration. Also, it was something that could be easily done.

'Indeed, racing driver Johnny Lurani told me that the reason all the cars in the 'entry level' Formula Junior single-seat class became Ford-engined was because it was the only engine with a truly unburstable bottom end that was available off the shelf in Europe.'

Highway Patrol: the West Sussex Police used a fleet of Lotus-Cortinas as high-speed pursuit cars. Because they carried so much extra electrical equipment, the standard dynamos were replaced with alternators. At high speeds, the vibration used to cause the alternator brackets to fracture.

Preparing upholstery hides in the PTA plant at Dagenham, which produced finished seats. Other interior trim items like headlinings, door panels and seats were produced in the River Plant and transferred to the PTA building for final assembly. The Dagenham plant used some 15 million sq ft of upholstery materials each year.

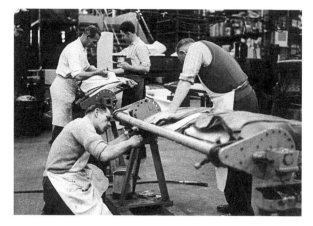

Leading the way in developing the Kent engine as a racing unit was a young Lancastrian engineer named Keith Duckworth, who had established his own engine tuning company with a friend named Mike Costin (who was then working for the recently-formed Lotus Cars) and called it 'Cosworth'.

When Hayes began seeking to add excitement to the Cortina, Duckworth was called in to develop a new camshaft for a performance version of the Cortina to be showcased at that fateful management appraisal at Montlhéry. The choice of the 'GT' label for this sporty Cortina, recalled Hayes, was lucky chance 'because we sent somebody to Halfords to find the prettiest badge to put on it. The prettiest badge he could find had "GT" on it, so we bought one.'

Dagenham's huge steel stockroom fed the factory's seemingly insatiable demand for sheet steel: in 1962, it consumed around 250,000 tons, plus another 80,000 tons of steel in bars and billets.

The GT soon represented 25 per cent of all Cortina production, recalled Hayes: 'It was an enormous success. This splendid performance sedan was a new concept in the marketplace, but it became perfectly obvious (to me anyway) that it wasn't enough and a "super GT" was obviously needed because the competitors were

beginning to nibble at us.'

Hayes called on his old friend Colin Chapman, who 'was frankly a bloody marvellous ideas man, the only ace motoring man I knew when I joined Ford. I'd paid him so much money as a journalist that I sometimes think I started Lotus!'

Left: An expert 'ding-man' rectifies slight imperfections in a car body as it proceeds down the assembly line.

Right: Final inspection for a new Ford as it reaches the end of the assembly line. The fitting of front seat belts became compulsory in Britain in 1967, though as early as 1955 Ford had been the first company to offer front and rear seat belts as production-fitted options.

Chapman had already developed an ingenious twin overhead camshaft conversion for the 1500cc Ford Classic engine using a cylinder head designed by Harry Mundy, the technical editor of *Autocar* magazine, which boosted output from 59.5 to 105bhp. This engine was intended for the Lotus Elan sports car and the close ties that even then were developing between Ford and Lotus are underlined by the fact that the Elan was launched to the press in Ford's Central London showrooms during the October 1962 Motor Show, with the press photographs taken in Ford's newly-established Aveley photographic studio by Ford photographer Ken Denyer. And when Chapman and Hayes sat late into the night planning their 'Super GT', the new Lotus-Ford engine was the natural choice to power it. So a prototype 1500cc Lotus-engined Cortina was built.

Meanwhile, Keith Duckworth and Mike Costin were called in to develop the Lotus-Ford engine for saloon car racing, then derive a production version. Toward this end, they changed all the engine ports and increased capacity from 1498 to 1558cc, since the new car would be running in the 1600cc class. Ford originally called the car 'the new high-powered Consul Cortina developed by Lotus,' but it quickly became known as 'Lotus-Cortina'.

Chapman's modifications to the Cortina were fundamental. The two-door bodyshells were fitted with light-alloy bootlids, bonnets and door skins. Clutch and differential housings were aluminium as well. A close-ratio Lotus gearbox, lowered

Finished cars were tested for leaks in an artificial rainstorm before being passed as ready for delivery to the Ford-Britain network of 2,000 domestic and 5,000 overseas dealerships.

front suspension and a totally new coil spring rear suspension layout with an A-frame mounted on the differential housing to control axle torque were other unique features.

Ford engineer George Baggs, who worked with Lotus to develop the prototype for quantity production, recalled: 'The object was to homologate the car, get it on the track to win races and get the maximum publicity out of it. So Chapman was given more or less a free hand to redesign it. And of course it upset the manufacturing people quite a bit because they had to provide the bodies, and all the modifications to the bodies obviously tended to disrupt production; there were so many special panels and so many extra brackets welded on to the car.

'They weren't used to this sort of work in the Dagenham plant, and they didn't actually welcome it, but our job was to smooth things out and keep the job going. You can imagine introducing things like alloy body panels into a mass-production plant!'

Ford had investigated the possibility of building complete Lotus-Cortinas at Dagenham, but concluded that it would be impractical, so the Dagenham bodyshells were transported to the new Lotus plant at Cheshunt, Hertfordshire, simultaneously moving from the world of mass-production into a cottage industry where cars were assembled by hand on trestles.

Dagenham's facilities underwent another phase of renewals during the 1960s as a new blast furnace capable of producing 750 tons of pig iron a day went into service and the Thames foundry, opened at a cost of £7.5 million as recently as 1957, was gutted and extended.

To make way for new production facilities, 300,000 square feet of balconies were removed from the Dagenham plant during 1954. The redevelopment had the added benefit of improving lighting in the previously gloomy plant.

Mk II Cortinas await collection on the quayside at Newark, New Jersey. The huge freighter ship was capable of carrying up to 1,200 cars in a single shipment.

Recalled Bill Camplisson, then in Ford product planning: 'Chapman said "You bring in painted, trimmed bodies on the back of a truck and back it up to this hole in the wall. I'll have six lads here with slings and pieces of 4x2 timber and we'll lift the body up, carry it into the middle of the warehouse and prop it up on some beer crates to give us room for some of the lads to crawl underneath and do a bit of assembly. Then we'll drop in the engine and the gearbox and bolt up the axle and the wheels and roll the cars out through the hole in the other side of the warehouse."'

The 'A-frame' rear suspension, originally designed for track racing, became a source of deep concern, for it concentrated all the driving loads into the centre of the standard Cortina axle, which duly bent and lost all its oil. *Autocar* Sports Editor Peter Garnier had an early Lotus-Cortina and loved it dearly, despite its appetite for crown wheels and pinions which made it such a frequent visitor to Cheshunt that the magazine's accountants eventually demanded its disposal. Years after, Lotus PR man Graham Arnold admitted that the entire car was rebuilt every time it came back for an axle service!

Nevertheless, the Lotus-Cortina caused a sensation when it was launched in January 1963, over two months ahead of the Cortina GT, which had been developed first. It was the fastest-ever British Ford, with a top speed of 108mph, and it only came in one colour scheme – white with a green sideflash and Lotus badges.

But the Lotus-Cortina was no bargain-basement performance car: at £1,110, it was the most expensive British Ford apart from the estate car versions of the big Zephyr and Zodiac, costing almost £300 more than rival Vauxhall's go-faster VX4/90.

However, despite its quirks and foibles and limited production run of just 3,301 units (against almost 77,000 GT Cortinas), the Lotus-Cortina gave Ford's image a valuable boost, recalled former Ford PR man and rally driver Gunnar Palm: 'This vehicle did more for Ford Motor Company than we estimated at the time. It transformed a company that had previously only produced bread-and-butter cars and gave it a sporting image.'

Walter Hayes made the most of the Lotus-Cortina's racetrack successes in the hands of top Grand Prix drivers like Jim Clark and Graham Hill: 'The Lotus-Cortina taught us a great deal about the growth of the youth performance market and brought a lot of people into motor sport who might not have been interested otherwise.'

But the problems engendered by the knife-and-fork production methods of Chapman's Cheshunt operation ensured that when a Mk II Cortina came along in 1966, the Lotus version was less radical and was built at Dagenham rather than by Lotus, even though that company had moved to a new factory at Hethel in Norfolk.

Moreover, Hayes's relationships with Cosworth and Lotus saw the creation of a new Cosworth Grand Prix engine that gave Ford domination of Formula One for a decade. Recalled Harry Calton: 'Walter's powers of persuasion were legendary. His joint presentation with engineering director Harley Copp to gain approval for the Ford F1 engine programme was covered under 'any other business' and took just nine minutes. But, as he stated afterwards, Ford had invested £1.25 million to add a synchromesh first gear to the Cortina while for just £250,000 they got world championship-winning F1 and F2 engines.'

Despite the ambitious expansion programme, by the early 1960s the growth in the British market meant that Dagenham was again running out of production space. Ford-Britain remained essentially the private domain of Sir Patrick Hennessy, who, although he had relinquished his executive functions at Ford-Britain in 1963, the year in which Dagenham exported its three millionth vehicle, was still chairman of the board. He was seeking backing for a major expansion of capacity to a maximum daily output of 4,300 cars, vans and trucks a day and talking of the possibility of moving to an additional production site.

Since Ford in Britain had long been synonymous with Dagenham, Sir Patrick was reluctant to consider moving far from the company's Essex base. However, government policy now dictated that Ford should locate any major new assembly plant in an area where unemployment was high.

The choices on offer were scarcely attractive to the autocratic Hennessy – they included Tyneside, South Wales and Scotland – but finally he chose the 'least worst' compromise at Halewood in Merseyside, 200 miles from Dagenham and only a short drive from Manchester, where Ford had begun manufacturing in Britain in 1911. The brand-new Halewood factory, capable of building 1,000 vehicles a day, opened on a 328-acre site in October 1963 at a cost of around £30 million. It had been the biggest expansion in the history of Ford in Britain, yet the move had been comparatively painless, thanks to an advanced training programme which began on New Year's Day 1962 in a hangar at Liverpool Airport fitted up as a factory in miniature.

For a similar reason, when in 1965 a new transmission plant began producing the rear axles that had formerly been made at Dagenham, it was located in a former

Ron Platt *(left)* responsible for selling British Fords in the USA, talks to Ford-Britain chairman Sir Patrick Hennessy on the company's stand at the New York Motor Show. Between them is former journalist John Dugdale, who represented Britain's motor industry in the United States and Canada.

domestic appliances factory at Swansea. In 1964 tractor production had also left Dagenham (which had built its millionth tractor two years before), though in this case it had moved only a few miles, to the Essex new town of Basildon.

But Dagenham still retained its 'self-contained' role as a major production plant. In 1964 its foundry operations had been relocated to an extended Thames Foundry and the power station produced enough electricity – 2 million kW hours a day – to supply a town with 160,000 inhabitants.

Sadly for Ford, industrial relations were a major problem at Dagenham (as, indeed, elsewhere in the growing Ford empire) in the 1960s. Union officials were supposed to obtain management approval before calling meetings on company premises, and when a Dagenham shop steward called a meeting without that permission in 1962 he was dismissed, even though the meeting had taken place during the lunch break. An unofficial strike resulted, and Allen Barke again used this as the reason for dismissing a number of known troublemakers.

This led to the threat of an official strike early in 1963 and the Ministry of Labour set up an official Court of Enquiry headed by Professor Jack, which suggested the setting up of a six-man negotiating committee to replace the existing National Joint Negotiating Committee, which had a member from each of the 22 unions recognised by Ford.

That didn't happen: and when in 1971 Ford was put out of action for 11 weeks, with the loss of 150,000 vehicles and £100 million, Dearborn abandoned its plan to build a new engine factory in Britain and Henry Ford II remarked: 'The labour situation has got to be cleaned up, otherwise our customers will go elsewhere.'

However, the volatile labour situation continued during the 1970s, with particular emphasis on pay and conditions, with Ford becoming regarded as the industry benchmark.

A new Mk II version of the Cortina had been launched in 1966 and became Britain's best-selling car in 1967; indeed, like every mark of the Cortina, it would go on to sell over a million units. That year, more Cortinas were sold abroad than any other two British cars put together, and some of those exports were bartered for coffee, cotton, potatoes and toilet seats! A strong sales campaign was run in the United States, and 200 American Ford dealers arrived in London in January 1967 to draw up plans for a major US sales drive for the new Cortina.

In February a new Cortina Estate was launched and the Mk II version of the Lotus Cortina appeared in March. Though production of the Mk II Lotus Cortina remained small, the model gave rise to one of the truly classic Fords of the 1960s, the 1600E. This characterful "executive express" was created by a group of

As this publicity photograph of the Hong Kong Police shows, the Mk II Cortina sold well in the far east: it was even assembled from 'knocked-down' kits in the Philippines.

enthusiastic product planners using the new crossflow 1600 GT engine announced in September 1967, Lotus Cortina suspension, wide-rimmed Rostyle wheels, a painted coachstripe, a leather-rimmed steering wheel and a luxury interior with a wooden dashboard made by a company that also made dashboards for Rolls-Royce. The 1600E remained in production until 1970 and some 58,000 were built.

It's a reflection on the way that standards of durability testing were changing at that period that it was regarded as a novelty that the pre-production programme for the new 1300 and 1600cc crossflow engines had included fitting them in 25 employees' Cortinas for extended 'family car running'.

Dagenham was perhaps getting too adventurous with colours: the most popular choices for 1967 were Blue Mink and Silver Fox metallics, which accounted for 40 percent of Cortina sales, with Saluki Bronze a close third: fresh out of the showroom these shades looked sensational, but when they were exposed to sunlight, they proved less than durable...

At around the same time as the Halewood project was under way, another way of increasing production capacity presented itself when the Rootes Group ran into financial problems. Founded as a cycle agency in Kent in the 19th century, Rootes had been one of the first specialist motor agents and when the makes which it represented began running into financial difficulties in the late 1920s, snapped up those which took its fancy. By the end of the 1950s, Rootes – still under family control – owned the archetypically British Humber, Hillman, Singer and Sunbeam-Talbot marques, and was seeking to expand its production facilities.

To accommodate its 'Project Ajax' – the new Hillman Imp minicar – Rootes rashly built a brand-new factory at Linwood in Scotland, where no other major

manufacturer dared locate a car plant. Dismal industrial relations and a reputation for poor build quality doomed the new car. Rootes recorded a loss in 1962–63, and never even got halfway toward its projected annual production of 150,000 Imps.

Nevertheless, Rootes, with its excellent dealer network and 8–10 per cent share of the British market, attracted Sir Patrick Hennessy, who saw the purchase as a simple way to obtain clear market leadership. Although Hennessy had a unique rapport with Henry Ford II, even he could not buy a company as big as Rootes without approval from World Headquarters in America. Consequently, Dearborn's top finance man Arjay Miller and his team moved into Ford's company flat in Grosvenor House in Park Lane. At first, their analysis seemed favourable to the deal. But the night before Henry Ford II was to meet Lord Rootes and conclude the deal, Miller realised that buying Rootes, with its poor management and huge overdraft, would be a risky distraction, and wrote a series of bullet points against the deal on little memo cards, including the poor labour record of what Allen Barke called the 'disaffected shale workers' of Linwood.

Then he sat outside the door of Henry Ford's apartment until he heard his boss get up. While Ford was shaving, Miller convinced him to call off the deal. Shattered by this last-minute rejection, Rootes turned elsewhere for salvation and in July 1964 Chrysler took a substantial stakeholding. It was not enough: the Rootes situation worsened, and in 1967 the Wilson government allowed a full Chrysler takeover. That year, Rootes lost a record £10.5 million: a dispirited Chrysler sold its loss-making European operations to Peugeot in 1978.

Arjay Miller's gut feeling had saved the normally astute Sir Patrick from making a costly mistake.

Chapter Nine

INTO THE
MELTING POT

OVER three decades after his new office block at Warley had opened in 1964 to accommodate some 2,000 central office staff transferred from Dagenham, and after he was long retired from Ford, Allen Barke was still inordinately proud of the building. However, at the time the bluff Lancastrian who was being groomed to succeed Sir Patrick Hennessy had little time to enjoy the new six-storey headquarters of Ford-Britain, for fate was to strike him a cruel blow.

Barke was in the habit of lunching on sandwiches made from wholemeal bread from his local bakery. For some inexplicable reason, the van delivering the flour one fateful day at the beginning of 1965 was also carrying a bag of glass fibre resin powder, and somehow some of the resin got into the flour without being noticed.

After eating a sandwich made with the contaminated bread, Barke was violently ill, so ill that he almost died, and although he eventually recovered and lived well into his eighties, his Ford career was ended and he was never able to exercise his new appointment as vice-chairman.

He was succeeded by American-born Stanley Gillen, a keen amateur horologist who had joined Ford in 1947 and risen to the chairmanship of Ford's British subsidiary Autolite, a 1962 acquisition formerly known as Simms Motor Units. Long-time manufacturing director Andy Taylor additionally became deputy managing director.

The carefully-considered role of the new Warley building as headquarters of the British Ford company was about to be thrown into the melting pot, along with the new £10.5 million research and engineering centre that was nearing completion a few miles down the road near the village of Dunton.

The fact that Britain and Germany were still going their own separate ways in most respects concerned the head of Ford-Germany, a tall bespectacled Californian named John Andrews. He wondered whether the lower development costs of launching a single European Ford family car in 1962 would have resulted in greater sales.

When in 1961 the United Kingdom decided to apply for full membership of the European Economic Community, Andrews asked one of his staff to prepare a report on the future state of Europe's trading relationships.

This marked the first step in 'Project Titus', in which Ford-International, working through Andrews, sought to see how a combined Ford organisation could operate within a common European market. There were, thought Andrews, three possible ways forward: 'Dagenham and Cologne continue to offer their present or planned product lines and continue to compete with each other; Dagenham and Cologne continue with separate product lines but agree not to compete with each other; only one product line is offered.'

Project Titus also discussed the future shape of product planning, engineering, manufacturing, purchasing and marketing – should these continue as separate functions at Dagenham and Cologne or be carried out by a new, centralised organisation?

Andrews suggested that Ford-Britain's managing director Charles Thacker, the Dagenham production man who had put Cologne back on its feet at the end of the war, should compile a 'study of studies' for further discussion. Thacker's report reviewed the advantages of merging the separate corporate functions carried out by Britain and Germany, but was firmly biased in favour of Britain. It suggested housing a central European staff at Warley.

'Although external competition between Dagenham and Cologne products may be discontinued, competition between the two plants in obtaining the maximum efficiency will continue.'

Memories of the war were still fresh, and Andrews noted that there could be reluctance in Britain to buy German cars 'and vice versa – for a period of time'. For that reason, Andrews tended to favour the retention of separate product ranges – what he called the 'two fishing line' approach. Nevertheless, he ordered his senior managers to list possible areas of coordination between Dagenham and Cologne.

The first of these to become reality was 'Project Redcap', a 1961 proposal for a common van design to replace Dagenham's 400E Thames and the German Taunus Transit. At first the two companies decided to continue developing their van replacements independently, since Britain was not going to enter the Common Market in the near future. A joint engineering programme thus offered little potential for cost saving since light commercials generally used passenger car components – and British and German passenger cars were far from identical.

But when Cologne revealed its proposed forward control Redcap design – codenamed for a small American bird rather than a military policeman – the Germans were told to examine anew the possibility of working on a joint van project with Ford-Britain.

The Germans were only too happy to fall in with this suggestion, recalled Allen Barke: 'The common van suited John Andrews more than it suited me, because Cologne did not have a good van whereas we already had the 800E van on the stocks to succeed the 400E. Nevertheless, we fell in with Andrews' suggestion that we join

Bizarrely, though the formation of Ford-Europe had been aimed at eliminating internecine competition between the British and German Ford companies, the Dagenham and Cologne versions of the 'TC' differed in styling and this Cortina is destined for Scandinavia to sell against its Taunus sibling.

forces for a brand new van and aimed for a universal design, a van of many parts and varieties. The customer could have any specialist vehicle, the design was so flexible.'

Moreover, a jointly-produced van would solve one of Ford-Germany's perennial problems. Cologne had no on-site bodybuilding facilities and had to rely on Drauz, a local coachbuilder who could not make enough van bodies to satisfy demand. The Redcap programme would overcome this shortfall.

While the two companies still considered themselves rivals, nevertheless, 18 months later Britain and Germany jointly presented their 'Study for a Common Van' to Ford's central operating policy committee. It proposed a new Redcap combining the semi-forward control layout of the British Thames van replacement (whose basic design was well under way) with the compact 1.7-litre V4 engine being developed for the 1964 Taunus.

The joint programme would allow direct comparison of work standards and cost performance in Britain and Germany and reduce costs by 'economies of scale' in component purchase and more efficient sourcing of exports. It would also give valuable experience for future common programmes, as Ford-International confidently predicted, 'the outlook was bright for Britain to join the Common Market in one manner or another prior to 1970'.

Nevertheless, the joint programme revealed unforeseen difficulties: 'Literal translations oftentimes lost the intent of comments and written communications,' ran a management report. 'Vestiges of former hostilities are minimal as compared to the basic differences between the two peoples and their associated lines of reasoning, communication and manner of doing things.'

The problems were hammered out by Allen Barke and a Dagenham team travelling to Cologne one month, with a return visit to Dagenham by John Andrews and his particular experts the following month. The new van, taking the name 'Transit' from its Cologne forebear, proved a resounding success. When it came to adding up the bills at the end of the development programme, there was a saving of more than $15 million – approximately 32 per cent compared with the previous system.

Dagenham learned many lessons: 'It was the first time we were required to produce bilingual engineering information', recalled British Redcap team member Fred Ray. 'At Dagenham we had to pick up the metric system so we had complete duplication. There was conflict as to the way the thing should be designed and manufactured.'

And, recalled Allen Barke in 1989, 'When we'd finished the van, John looked at it from his point of view, and I looked at it from mine, and neither of us liked it!'

Nevertheless, when the Transit was launched in 1965, it immediately became

Like its predecessors, the Mk III Cortina sold over a million examples. It certainly kept Dagenham's production lines busy, for it was marketed in 35 basic versions.

Britain's best-selling commercial vehicle, exceeding all management estimates. It has maintained that lead ever since, an unparalleled success in the British new vehicle market. But the very success of the Redcap programme was to reduce Dagenham's place in the Ford scheme of things yet further.

An internal report said that despite the problems encountered in bringing the Common Van Programme to fruition, it had revealed the potential benefits of greater cooperation between Britain and Germany. It recommended 'greater standardisation between the two organisations', particularly in engineering and financial control, even though 'there is little inclination at this time to cooperate more closely with each other.

'We strongly recommend the establishment of a separate product group comprised of capable bilingual personnel from both locations to develop and coordinate future common programmes.'

Eventually, said the report, a 'supra-national product group' should be evolved, in which differences in nationality would tend to play a far smaller role. 'Although substantially greater differences exist between Ford of Britain and Ford of Germany than exist between the two domestic vehicle divisions, we are convinced these differences are not insurmountable.'

Allen Barke, who thought internal competition was an effective marketing method, disagreed: 'We do not believe that a customer denied the opportunity of purchasing a Ford Germany product will necessarily purchase a Ford Britain product or vice versa; he may equally well buy a Volkswagen, Renault or Fiat.'

But with Barke out of the picture and Sir Patrick Hennessy on the brink of

A full-width aluminium grille and 'gunsight' bonnet motif distinguished the 1968 Zephyr V6 De Luxe from its humbler siblings.

retirement, Henry Ford II decided that the merits of cooperation outweighed those of competition.

In Paris for a management meeting, he called an impromptu meeting in his suite at the Plaza Athenée hotel with Andrews of Ford-Germany, Gillen of Ford-Britain and British public affairs director Walter Hayes, who had become Mr Ford's confidant. As Hayes recalled many years later, 'It was all terribly informal. Mr Ford said that he had decided that the time had come to create a Ford of Europe organisation and told John Andrews: 'You are going to be in charge; get it going! There's no sense in worrying about Dearborn – it's a European operation and I want to see it put together.'

Anyone who was involved at the beginning of Ford of Europe recalls the speed with which the organisation sprang into existence. The choice of Warley as the central offices of Ford of Europe proved inevitable. Though Brussels was favoured by Andrews, it was a non-starter as far as Americans seconded to the new organisation were concerned. Not only did a British posting offer them significant tax advantages, American Ford executives and their families tended to be 'congenitally monolinguistic'.

The British management, whose new office building represented a solution to the chronic overcrowding at Dagenham, certainly hadn't envisioned sharing its imposing headquarters with another organisation. Since Ford-Britain had also just opened its new Dunton research and development facility, it was obviously anticipating continuing to evolve dedicated models for the home market (as was Ford-Germany, which was building its own research and development centre at Cologne-Merkenich).

A pre-production Zodiac Mk IV framed by the pride of the BOAC fleet, the four-jet VC-10 airliner. Quad headlamps were a recognition feature.

Nevertheless, the omens for Warley were propitious. Over a century earlier, the site had been the barracks of the East India Company – perhaps the first successful 'multinational' – and the directors' garage was built where they had once stabled the elephants used to teach young officers basic pachyderm management in

Making a splash: prototype Zephyrs and Zodiacs were flown to Lebanon in December 1965 for pre-launch photography with the 'cosmopolitan atmosphere of Beirut' as a backdrop.

the incongruous setting of the Essex countryside.

The difficulties of fusing two entirely separate organisations disrupted many careers, particularly on the engineering side. One British manager recalled: 'People given no real alternative but to take early retirement; their lives were shattered – there were grown men crying in their offices.'

One of the main losers was Ford-Britain's American director of engineering Harley Copp, a larger-than-life character often seen at the wheel of a Rolls-Royce which had been acquired by Ford at his behest for 'product appraisal'. Copp and his executive engineer George Halford had been responsible for the last of the Zephyr/Zodiac line, the Mk IV range launched in 1966 which, at Copp's request, had been larger than its predecessors, with similar dimensions to the contemporary American Ford Fairlane. Neat 'bow-back' styling by Charles Thompson made the capacious boot look deceptively short. New Dagenham-built compact V4 and V6 'Essex' engines were used, with the forward part of the large bonnet area occupied by the spare wheel.

While Copp had insisted on independent rear suspension, the chosen design was prone to alarming 'tuck-under' of the outer rear wheel when cornering with empty back seats.

Since Germany had only two car product lines to Britain's four, Copp had

The Zodiac Mk IV was a capacious load-carrier, with a rear deck large enough to be used as an ambulance.

With a distinctive 'Lincoln Star' grille emblem, the luxurious Executive was based on the Zodiac. It was the first car to be fitted as standard with inertia-reel seat belts on all four seats: prestige marques like Mercedes and Jaguar still regarded seat belts as an aftermarket fitting.

assumed that he would get the top job – but it went to his opposite number Jack Hooven – another American – in Cologne.

Perhaps, then, it was inevitable that the first true 'European' project – the 'Mk III' version of the Cortina, to be built in Germany under the 'Taunus' label – should be an uncomfortable compromise with more than its fair share of teething troubles. The engineering team, initially led by Harley Copp and later – when Copp had returned to the US – by Fred Piziali, had created an all-new chassis using the all-new 'Pinto' engine range, with cogged belt drive to a single overhead camshaft, that possessed troublesomely erratic wearing properties.

The 'TC', as it was known within Ford, was a monument to the cussedness of Harley Copp, for it had his preferred coil-spring and wishbone 'SLA' ('short and long arm') front suspension, which was a step backwards compared with the original Cortina's MacPherson Strut. Its bodywork was a miniature of the American baroque styling then favoured in Dearborn, with a pronounced 'coke-bottle' kick-up over the rear wheels and difficult-to-press ridges extending the front wing tips forward to frame a 'more prestigious' grille incorporating – according to model – twin or quad

The Mk IV range went into production at Dagenham after a five-year gestation period which had begun on 10 February 1971 – over a year before the launch of the Mk III range – when Ford's eight-man Product Committee began the first studies for a new large car which would be codenamed 'Project Panda'.

headlamps. The styling of the Mk III Cortina definitely had more of a 'Detroit look' than its predecessors.

Strangely for the vision of European unity, the Cologne version used different external sheet metal, as though the old 'two fishing lines' approach still held good.

Nevertheless, the new Cortina, launched in late 1970, was a resounding success and – like the two preceding marks, sold over a million. In fact, at the end of 1972, the Cortina Mk III had outsold all other cars on the British market in each month and its overall sales of 187,159 were a new Ford record.

Despite the high sales, every Cortina coming down the line at Dagenham was built to an individual specification, whether for a particular customer order or for a dealer's sales stock. A curious feature of the Dagenham production dockets in those pre-hatchback days was that the same telegraphese nomenclature was used

This 'Heath Robinson' device compressed the rear quarters of Mk III Cortinas intended for Japan, where cars were taxed on width, to bring them within a cheaper tax bracket. 'Rejects' were recycled for domestic consumption!

Ford was engaged in many astute publicity ventures in the 1960s, including this inspired 'rescue operation' in 1970 to bring a 1930s Hawker Hind biplane home from Afghanistan to be restored to flying condition by the Shuttleworth Trust.

The architect of the Ford-Europe plan for a common market of the motor industry was American John Andrews *(right)*, seen greeting his boss Henry Ford II. Mr Ford railroaded the plan through in an impromptu meeting in his suite at the Plaza Athenée hotel, while in Paris for a management meeting.

to identify bodyshells as had been the Ford rule since the days of the Model T – 'Tudor' denoted a two-door car, 'Fordor' a four-door.

Because Japan has the same rule of the road as Britain, the small number of European Fords sold there were shipped from Dagenham rather than Cologne. However, the Japanese road tax system was based on width because so many Japanese roads were so narrow, and the standard Mk III bodyshell was marginally too wide across the rear wheel arches to slot into a particular tax bracket. The ingenious workers on the body line at Dagenham devised a 'Heath Robinson' device which could be fitted between the rear wheel arches of a bodyshell before it received its final welds and tightened up by opposite-threaded screws to pull the wheel arches together by the requisite amount. Tack welds were then applied to hold the bodyshell at the right setting: if it sprang back too far when the screw device was removed, it was just put back on the line for domestic consumption, and no-one was any the wiser.

From being the centre of all Ford activity in Europe, Dagenham had become a nest from which the high-flyers had flown, a process speeded by the seismic reaction to the formation of Ford-Europe. Many senior managers simply 'voted with their feet'; six months after the foundation of Ford-Europe, Walter Hayes – shortly to become Ford-Europe's first director of public affairs – wrote to his boss in Dearborn: 'The "brain drain" from Ford in Europe continues… Ford of Britain has, in the past day or two lost four good senior management people to the new British Leyland group, including the manager of production planning and control (a first class man).

'When the production man's outside appointment was announced, he had a dozen phone calls from people inside the company saying, "Can we come too?" Obviously when these men are established in the new British Leyland group they will take other men from here.

'Moreover, the drift of Ford men to this True Blue rival gives them an enormous depth of inside knowledge about our operations and plans. A sales meeting for British Leyland dealers in Brussels last week was held by four executives, every one of whom two months ago worked for Ford.

'These attitudes are understandable because the effect of the Ford of Europe reorganisation has been to appear to demote just about everybody involved.'

Nevertheless, Britain and Germany were working together on the first truly common car programme, developing the smoothly-styled 1972 Consul/Granada range that was to replace one of Harley Copp's more idiosyncratic designs, the Mk IV Zephyr/Zodiac line. But that was a day that John Andrews did not see. Even before he had taken over as the first chairman of Ford of Europe he had been diagnosed as having leukaemia and in 1969 he could no longer carry on working. Shortly after taking sick leave, John Andrews died.

Chapter Ten

DECLINE AND FALL

FROM the mid-1960s it was possible for a British Ford employee to spend his entire working life with the company without ever visiting Dagenham. Yet even though all its senior management functions had been dissipated, Dagenham was still the focus of Ford-Britain's car and engine production, with the Mk III Cortina and Mk IV Zephyr Zodiac range briefly supplemented in 1969–70 by the 'run-out' of the Corsair line, which had been transferred south from Halewood. In 1970–72 the Engine Plant was enlarged from 1.8 million to 2.5 million square feet to accommodate production of overhead camshaft petrol and direct-injection diesel engines.

Dagenham's last large car line was the 1972 Consul/Granada range. This production line shot shows how the bodyshell was mated to the complete engine/front suspension assembly.

Spot-welding the floorpan of a Granada still involved much manual labour, even though Ford was moving toward automation of the process.

However, production of the Mk IV Zephyr Zodiac range had fallen steadily from the first full year, 1967, in which 50,593 cars were built. In 1970 the figure was only 18,925 and in 1971, the last year of manufacture, output was almost exactly one-third of the first year's figure.

The successor to the Mk IV range, the 1972 Consul/Granada, graphically underlined the decline of Dagenham as the centre of the European Ford universe, for the new cars were designed in Cologne under the code designation 'MH'. This oddly enough stood for 'Medium Hummer' ('Hummer' is German for lobster) and the new cars – to be built in both Dagenham and Cologne – were made slightly more compact than the Mk IV under the slogan 'brings large cars down to size'.

The limitations of the new 'one size fits all' European philosophy were graphically illustrated when the acquisition of the Ghia studio in Italy was celebrated by the 1974 flagship 'Granada Ghia' range (though it had been styled in Cologne rather than Turin.). Among the Ghia models was the Cologne-built two-door Granada Ghia Coupé, a fastback five-seater. While such saloon-derived coupés represented a significant part of the Granada market in Germany, where most Granadas were owner-driven, many British Granadas were chauffeur-driven, so four-door models were preferred.

The model 'bombed' on the British market to such an extent that dealers were forced to take one Granada Ghia Coupé for every ten of the popular Cortina range they ordered, so many of the difficult-to-sell Ghia Coupés ended up as executive transport for the dealer principals!

An impressive feature of the production process at Dagenham was the multi-point welding jig in which body panels placed in a 'framing buck' were transformed into a complete bodyshell by a battery of automatic spot welding heads working to unprecedented standards of accuracy.

In 1975 the Consul name was laid to rest, and all models became known as 'Granada'. This was Dagenham's last big Ford, for in July 1976 all Granada production was transferred to Germany since the British output had fallen away dramatically.

When production at Dagenham resumed after the 1976 summer break, the plant's mainstay was the sleek new Mk IV Cortina range, which – like Kipling's 'Colonel's lady and Judy

Ford's stands at the Motor Show have long been a meeting place for the great and good. Here Princess Anne meets Formula One World Champion Jackie Stewart *(centre)* and Ken Tyrrell, constructor of Stewart's winning Ford-Cosworth-engined car, at the 1971 Earls' Court Show.

Ford Capri

A Mk IV Consul leaves the assembly line. Falling demand caused the end of Consul/Granada production at Dagenham in July 1976 after 123,368 units had been built, though it continued at Cologne for another year.

Left: Dagenham management admire the plant's first Fiesta early in 1977. Though they could not know it, the Fiesta was to become the Thames-side plant's mainstay in years to come.

Right: The Mk IV Cortina was a skilful 'reskinning' of the old Mk III by the design team headed by the urbane Uwe Bahnsen. At last British and German versions looked the same, though the cars from Cologne still carried the Taunus name.

O'Grady' – was sister under the skin to the Mk III line. The existing underpinnings had been skilfully reclad by the Cologne design studios headed by the urbane Uwe Bahnsen, and the new look was common to both Dagenham-built Cortinas and Cologne's Taunus.

Ford-Britain's diehard chairman, Sir William Batty – who had joined Ford's Trade School in Manchester as an apprentice in 1930 – had liked the 'Coke-bottle' haunches of the Mk III range, and wanted to perpetuate the 'two fishing lines' philosophy in a Dagenham-only Cortina with the tail of the Mk III and the front end of the Taunus. To humour him, a 'Mk III/IV' hybrid was mocked up in the Dunton design studio and wheeled out during the coffee break of a management appraisal of prototypes. As the assembled managers gazed at this corporate camel, its driver's door mirror gradually drooped and fell to the floor with a loud clatter. That, thankfully, was the last seen of the hybrid Cortina.

A radically new model had been under development by Ford, which was anxious to establish a firm foothold in the expanding southern European market, with its emphasis on small economy cars. Despite the deeply entrenched wisdom of the motor industry – 'mini car, mini profits' – the new Fiesta was the company's first front-wheel drive car, the first with a transverse engine, and it had the smallest engine Ford had built since the 8hp Anglia had gone out of production in the 1950s. A new factory had been built at Valencia in Spain, where the previous Ford plant in Barcelona had closed as a direct result of the Civil War four decades earlier.

Fiestas for the British market were built at Dagenham. The power unit for the new model was derived from the 'Kent' series, with a new cylinder block that was more than an inch shorter and had only three main bearings. The Fiesta was launched in Britain in February 1977 and in March 1979 Dagenham produced a special edition model called the Fiesta Million, to mark the building of the millionth example of this phenomenally successful minicar.

However, Dagenham's role in the Ford scheme of things was declining, for the

A facelift for the Mk IV range came in August 1979 when a new grille with aerofoil slats and larger windows were introduced.

Every mark of Cortina sold more than a million: here Dagenham workers celebrate the building of the four millionth Cortina to leave the line since production began in September 1962.

In October 1981 Dagenham celebrated its Golden Jubilee with a reunion of survivors of the opening of the plant 50 years earlier.

At the age of 93 Sir Rowland Smith (left), chatting with 1981 chairman Sam Toy, was driven off the end of the assembly line by the author in this specially-restored Ford AA truck, to re-enact the production of Dagenham's first vehicle in 1931. Sir Rowland celebrated his 100th birthday before he died in 1988.

Cortina had been edged out of top place in the UK market by the more economical Halewood-built Escort in 1976 during the aftermath of the first big fuel shock. However, Cortina regained its top slot again the following year, and remained there until 1981, to be replaced the following year by the radically-different Sierra, with aerodynamic styling and all-round independent suspension.

When the top management of Ford-Europe was discussing the name for the Cortina's replacement, one director suggested that another popular European ski resort might be a good choice. 'Like Garmisch-Partenkirschen?' quipped Ford-Europe's chairman Bob Lutz.

Engine production continued to be a Dagenham mainstay: in January 1979 the plant produced its millionth Dorset Diesel engine, while a derivative design, the Dover, was launched two years later. Dagenham's position as Ford's sole European diesel engine plant was further enhanced by the 1984 launch of new 1.6-litre and 2.5-litre diesel engines.

To round off Cortina production, the Cortina Crusader appeared in May 1982, in a joint promotion with the *Daily Express*, whose symbol appeared on the bootlid. The last Cortina was driven off the Dagenham production line on 22 July 1982 by Ford-Britain's Chairman Sam Toy, who had joined Ford at Dagenham in

After 20 years and nearly 4.3 million cars, the last Cortina – one of the 'Crusader' special edition of 30,000 cars – was driven off the line by Ford chairman Sam Toy to join the company's collection of historic vehicles.

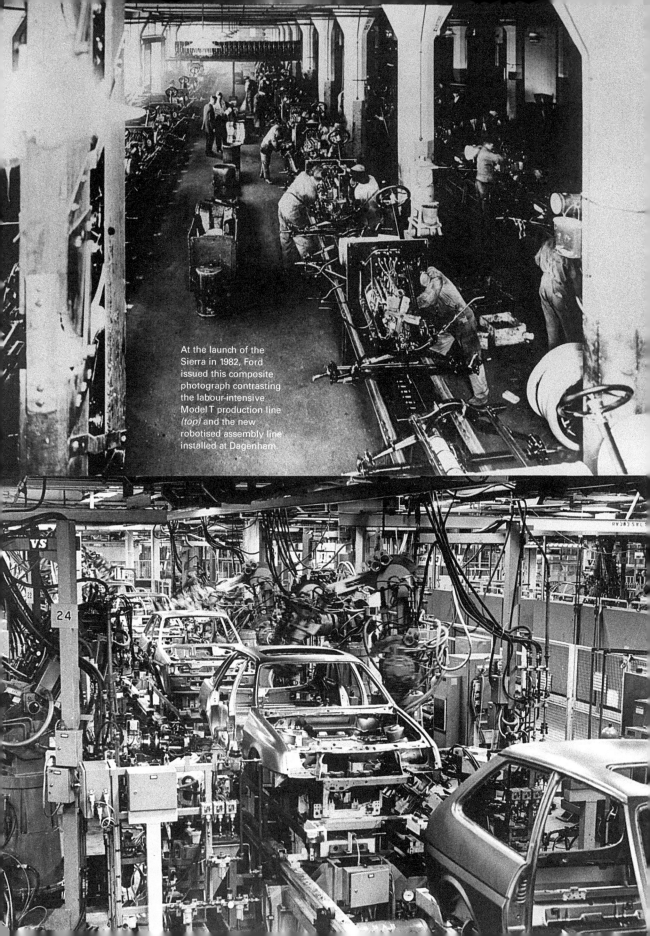

At the launch of the Sierra in 1982, Ford issued this composite photograph contrasting the labour-intensive Model T production line *(top)* and the new robotised assembly line installed at Dagenham.

1948 as one of its first graduate trainees after service flying Bristol Blenheims in the RAF.

The introduction of the Sierra caused many headaches at Dagenham, for the new model was designed for production by robots, and the new machinery needed far more headroom than had been allowed for by the architects of the old factory building. This meant going down into the floor to give sufficient overhead clearance for the robot arms: the bonus was that the robots did the job perfectly every time. Human error (and strikes) were eliminated.

Dagenham was more fortunate than its satellite factory at Cork in southern Ireland, where the volume of production was insufficient to warrant the installation of a robot line. Consequently the assembly of cars for the Irish market from 'knocked-down' kits sent from England came to an end after 60 years.

The new Dagenham robots were even programmed to spray bodyshells: this was where the ability of robots to work in hazardous conditions was of particular benefit. Once the robot arm had been taken through the correct sequence of operations by a skilled operator, it reproduced the movements of its human teacher perfectly, even changing the colours it sprayed between cars according to a pre-set computer program. Consequently, each robot seemed to develop a near-human personality.

Dagenham workers install the windscreen on an early Dagenham-built Sierra. Screens were now bonded in place rather than retained by a rubber grommet, adding to the structural strength of the bodyshell.

Sierra engine/front suspension assemblies advance down the Dagenham line like the work of a modern Sorcerer's Apprentice.

Left: Ford invested £210 million in new metal stamping and body manufacturing facilities at Dagenham for the introduction of the Sierra in 1982. This is the face-lifted 'Mk II' version on the line at Dagenham.

Right: Nearing the end of the line: less than 10 years from the major investment in new manufacturing plant for the launch of the Sierra, all Sierra production had been concentrated at the Cologne-controlled Genk plant in Belgium. Dagenham had become a one-model plant again for the first time since 1932.

A couple of years after the robots went on stream, a chapter in Dagenham history drew to a close when the Ford accountants decided that it would be cheaper to buy in castings rather than make their own. And so the Thames Foundry was closed and the site cleared, apart from the canteen building, which until the year 2000 (when it, too, was demolished) served as a visitor centre for plant tours and a home for the company's collection of historic vehicles.

While car production shrank to one model line in the 1990s when manufacture of the Mondeo – successor to the Sierra – was concentrated at Genk in Belgium, Dagenham continued as the main manufacturing plant for the Fiesta, and 'heavy investment' was made in updating its production facilities in the early 1990s. In mid-decade, Dagenham celebrated the production of its two-millionth Fiesta.

Major investments were also made in the engine plant, with £91 million being spent on improvements in diesel engine manufacturing technology to enable over 1,500 1.8-litre diesel engines to be built each day.

The plant's future as a car manufacturing centre seemed safe, even though employment at Dagenham had fallen from over 40,000 in 1963 to just 8,000 in 1996. 'Significant improvements' were made to the Dagenham manufacturing facilities when a new Fiesta made its debut in 1996, including fully-automated press shop lines with a body-side complex that reduced assembly tolerances to ensure more precise door fit. Instrument panels were pre-assembled off-line for increased reliability, with the instruments and switchgear checked for function before installation by an automated 'lazy arm'.

The process of trimming the painted bodyshell of a Fiesta gets under way in the early 1980s. The interior side panel trims are in place but the seats are not yet installed.

It all looked good, and when on 8 October 1996 Dagenham assembled its 20 millionth vehicle, it was also the parent Ford company's 250 millionth vehicle worldwide. The future looked so bright that it was announced that when a new Fiesta was launched, Dagenham would be the lead plant producing it, with the old foundry site developed as a supplier park furnishing components to the production line on a 'just-in-time' basis along similar lines to Ford's Valencia plant in Spain.

But the clouds of over-capacity had been gathering on the European horizon for some years, and fundamental changes were about to take place on the Dagenham site. The main office building had already lost the statue of Henry Ford I – one of only three in the world – which had been relocated in front of the heritage centre on the old foundry site, and at the end of 1997 it lost its office staff, too, and was left standing empty and forlorn.

The engine plant built its 30 millionth power unit on 17 September 1998 and in April the following year built its 4 millionth 1.6/1.8-litre diesel engine. But it was no longer the 'Detroit of Europe' and when in 1999 a new A13 trunk road was opened which swept across the centre of the Ford plant on stilts to link up with the M25 London Orbital motorway, it revealed the number of buildings that had been demolished on the once busy site.

The real bombshell fell in mid-February 2000, when, after production of the best-selling Fiesta had been on an effective four-day week for 18 months because of falling sales in Europe, Ford announced that it was to axe 1,500 workers at Dagenham. Production was to be downsized from two shifts to one, cutting daily output from 1,200 to around 560 units.

New faces on the line: changing patterns of employment meant that a significant proportion of the Dagenham workforce was female and there was an increasing number of workers from ethnic minorities. Said Ford: 'We take matters of equal opportunities and diversity extremely seriously.'

Left: Engine manufacture at Dagenham has become increasingly automated. Here engine blocks await the fitting of their pistons. Each set exactly matched to the cylinder bore.

Right: Fiesta 'bodies-in-white' pass through ostrich-feather rollers to remove static electricity which could attract dust and mar the finish.

Each bay in Dagenham's huge press shop is 'big enough to erect a ship'. The presses are arranged in sequence to maintain a steady production flow.

Worse was to follow. Ford announced in mid-May that production of the Fiesta would move to Cologne in 2002 and that Dagenham's paint, trim and assembly plant would close with the loss of 1,900 jobs. Dagenham was not the only victim of Ford's axe: newer plants in Poland, Belarus and Portugal were also to close.

In place of the Dagenham vehicle assembly plant, Ford began building a $500 million diesel engine complex with the necessary 'clean-room' conditions for building common-rail diesels, where tolerances are extremely fine and microscopic dust particles can foul minuscule injector ports. Working in partnership with the French PSA/Peugeot-Citroen group, Ford developed the new Lion V6 common-rail diesel engine, though the engine's designation proved which was the dominant

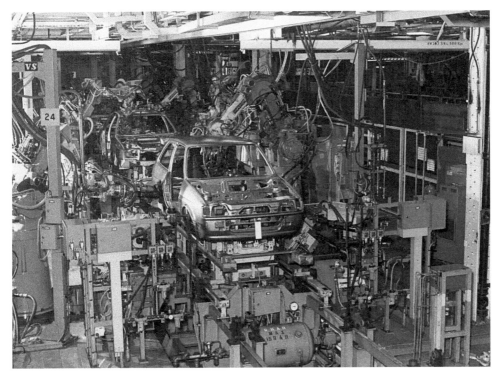

Welding robots at work on Fiesta bodyshells. Unveiling the 1996 version of the Fiesta, Ford proudly announced that 'Dagenham is Ford's lead manufacturing plant for the Fiesta, and has received heavy investment in updated facilities in recent years.'

partner in the development exercise, for the Lion of Belfort has been Peugeot's corporate symbol for over a century. The Lion engine was to be built at Dagenham for installation in future Jaguars and Volvos as well as mass-market Fords, Peugeots and Citroëns, for Jaguar and Volvo are part of Ford's Premier Automotive Group of luxury brands.

Ford was confident about Dagenham's long-term future, declaring: 'Ford Motor Company has had manufacturing facilities in Britain since 1911 and we remain committed to Britain's industrial, engineering and economic base.

'Ford Motor Company's automotive manufacturing and sales companies in Britain employ around 39,000 people. If Ford's other subsidiaries in Britain are included this figure is close to 48,000 people, making Ford the biggest employer in the British automotive industry. Even with the cessation of Fiesta production at Dagenham, Ford Motor Company will remain Britain's largest vehicle manufacturer in total.

'Over a million engines were manufactured by Ford Motor Company in Britain in 2000 – one in seven of all engines in Ford cars sold globally. By 2004, around two million diesel engines and petrol engines will be manufactured in Britain – one in four of all Ford engines built globally. The Ford Dagenham Diesel Business Centre is Ford's global centre of excellence for the engineering and manufacture of high quality technically-advanced diesel engines.

Painted Fiesta bodyshells proceed toward the final assembly area. During 1994 Ford built almost 194,000 Fiestas at Dagenham.

On 19 December 1996 the Dagenham Engine Plant produced its 29 millionth engine since production began in 1931. It was also the Engine Plant's 2 millionth 2.5-litre direct-injection diesel engine.

'Ford Motor Company has had a positive impact on the industrial, engineering, economic and social well-being of Britain throughout the 20th century. We fully intend to maintain the momentum in the 21st century.'

But where in the proud days of Sir Patrick Hennessy, Ford had boasted that Dagenham was the "heart of Ford of Britain", in the 21st Century it's just another Ford plant of many across Europe, with fewer employees than at any time in its history.

On 8 October 1996 boxer Frank Bruno was at Dagenham to drive its 10 millionth vehicle off the production line. It was also the 250 millionth vehicle produced by the worldwide Ford empire since Henry Ford built his first Model A in 1903.

A proud moment for the Dagenham Engine Plant came in December 1999 when it was presented with Ford's coveted Q1 quality award.

Car production at Dagenham finally came to an end on 20 February 2002, but the plant continues to play its part in Ford's European operations, though these are now run from Cologne rather than Warley. Its press shop continues stamping panels for Ford's Transit, Galaxy, S-Max, Mondeo, Focus, Fiesta and Ka ranges, and also produces panels for other companies within the Ford group: Mazda, Land Rover, Volvo, and Jaguar.

It is, too, a vital hub of engine production for the Ford group: in November 2003 Prime Minister Tony Blair opened the Dagenham Diesel Centre, a centre of excellence for diesel engineering. Together with the existing Dagenham engine plant, the DDC produces diesel engines for Ford, Land Rover and Jaguar cars, and at the time of writing the plants were on target to produce a million engines annually by the end of the decade.

Even though the Dagenham Heritage Centre no longer exists, the company still keeps its fleet of 96 historic vehicles at Dagenham, having taken over the old youth training scheme workshop in Kent Avenue to house them. Though the collection is not open to the public, most of the vehicles are road legal and can be seen in action at appropriate events.

A spectacular view of Ford's downsized operations at Dagenham can be obtained from the rerouted A13 highway, which now sweeps high over the northern end of the site that was once described as Ford's Thamesside "lighthouse of hope". Many of the buildings that once made this Britain's most self-sufficient car plant are gone, but Ford of Dagenham is still in production, three-quarters of a century after its opening. It may no longer be the Detroit of Europe, but in a radically-changed world motor industry, its mere survival is surely a matter for celebration.

INDEX

ND - #0335 - 270225 - C0 - 248/184/13 - PB - 9781780911366 - Gloss Lamination